Cycling in The Netherlands

The very best routes in a cyclist's paradise

Eric van der Horst

Cycling in The Netherlands
The very best routes in a cyclist's paradise

Published by CycleCity Guides, 2011
www.cyclecityguides.co.uk

ISBN: 978-1900623193

Photography by Ellen Brans, Dawn Connor, Eleanore Hamaker, Bert van der Horst, Eric van der Horst, Eric Keetels, Paul Marshall, Peter Tol and Dirk van Rens.

About the author

Cycling Dutchman Eric van der Horst has cycled all his life. His explorations within The Netherlands date back to his early teenage years. He went on his first cycling holiday when he was 16 and has covered most countries in Western Europe by bike. In his twenties, he cycled coast-to-coast in Australia and America and also cycled the full South Island of New Zealand. Today, he is a UK-based cycling professional, working as a cycle route surveyor, consultant and Bikeability instructor. He has written two books about cycling: one about his coast-to-coast ride in America and another on a long-distance cycle route from Harwich to Land's End (UK). Both books were published in Dutch – this book is his first to be published in the English language. For more information, check his cycling holiday company website www.eoscycling.com or www.cyclinginholland.com

Eric on a ride in The Netherlands

Contents

A key to symbols and abbreviations plus information on more cycling in The Netherlands can be found on the inside covers.

General information

Legend:
- Main route
- Links
- Northern route
- Eastern route
- Southern route
- Tulip Fields route
- → Direction of travel
- Route section (referring to page)
- Railway line & station (relevant lines & stations only)

Map labels:

Waddenzee
Den Helder
IJsselmeer
Markermeer
17 Horn - Enkhuizen
16 Volendam - Hoorn
Enkhuizen
Hoorn
Alkmaar
15 Amsterdam - Volendam
Lelystad
Zwolle
8 Haarlem - Amsterdam
Koog-Zaandijk
NETHERLANDS
1 Link Ijmuiden - Spaarndam
Santpoort Noord
Amsterdam Centraal
Almere
6 Overveen - Haarlem
Haarlem
Sloterdijk
Weesp
Zandvoort
Overveen
10 Amsterdam - Maarssen
Deventer
to Berlin
Schiphol Airport
Apeldoorn
Enschede
North Sea
7 Voorhout - Haarlem
9 Amsterdam - Extra Round
Hilversum
5 Water Tower - Overveen
Hollandsche Rading
Amersfoort
Voorhout
Breukelen
18 Maarssen - Soesterberg
4 Duindorp - Water Tower (The Hague)
Leiden
11 Maarssen - De Haar (Utrecht)
19 Soesterberg - Rhenen
3 Main Hook - Duindorp
13 Gouda - Delft
Woerden
Utrecht
Maarn
Arnhem
Den Haag Centraal
Delft
Gouda
Rhenen
Opheusden
Hoek van Holland - Haven
12 De Haar - Gouda
to Frankfurt
2 Link Hook -

North
Sea

NETHERLANDS

6 Overveen - Haarlem

Haarlem

Amsterdam
Centraal

Almere

Zandvoort

Overveen

Sloterdijk

Weesp

Deventer

Enschede

to Berlin

7 Voorhout - Haarlem

Schiphol
Airport

10 Amsterdam -
Maarssen

Apeldoorn

5 Water Tower -
Overveen

9 Amsterdam -
Extra Round

Hilversum

Voorhout

Leiden

Breukelen

Hollandsche Rading

18 Maarssen -
Soesterberg

4 Duindorp - Water Tower
(The Hague)

11 Maarssen -
De Haar (Utrecht)

Woerden

Amersfoort

19 Soesterberg -
Rhenen

3 Main Hook - Duindorp

13 Gouda -
Delft

Utrecht

Maarn

Arnhem

Den Haag -
Centraal

Delft

Gouda

Rhenen

Hoek van Holland -
Haven

12 De Haar -
Gouda

Opheusden

to Frankfurt

2 Link Hook -
Hull Terminal (Europoort)

14 Delft -
Hook

Rotterdam

Geldermalsen

Nijmegen

24 Goeree Landing -
Europoort

20 Rhenen -
Nijmegen

23 Breezand -
Goeree Landing

Haringvliet

Dordrecht

21 Nijmegen
& beyond

GERMANY

Grevelingen

Den Bosch

Oosterschelde

Breda

22 Vlissingen -
Breezand

Roosendaal

Tilburg

Vlissingen

to Antwerp

to Brussels

Eindhoven

Westerschelde

BELGIUM

Venlo

to Düsseldorf

to Maastricht

Introduction

Cycling in The Netherlands is a revelation. Not only do you have the run of 25,000 miles of traffic-free cycling routes on a flat terrain, you can also fully enjoy the benefits of a true cycling culture. You will be treated like a king of the road and can enjoy all those special cycling-minded traffic rules that Dutch cyclists take for granted.

Cycling in The Netherlands is for everyone, whether you are a novice cyclist or want to do some serious mileage. It is especially great for cycling with families, as distances are small and there is plenty of entertainment along the way. Children particularly love the cycle-path infrastructure with its own signage, introducing them to traffic participation in a perfectly safe environment. The routes in this guidebook can easily be cycled on a shopper, but if you wish to bring your racing bike with all the gears, that is very much possible as well!

With so many routes to choose from we decided to focus on those routes which are significant for the international visitor. All routes in this guidebook give you something extra. We guide you along those special landmarks, places of interest, the best countryside and most definitely the finest rides of the country.

To make navigating easy we decided on a circular route in central Netherlands, where you find a multitude of landscapes with plenty of possibilities for sightseeing. For those who want more, there are three additional one-way routes stretching north, east and south into the country. All these routes have their own particular character, different from the main route. To rejoin the main circular route or to skip route sections, you just hop on the train – see the overview map. The guide also offers a circular route in Amsterdam and a tulip fields route.

The main circular route has easy access from all Dutch main ferry ports such as Rotterdam Europoort (ferries from Hull), Hook of Holland (ferries from Harwich), and Amsterdam IJmuiden (ferries from Newcastle). You can also join the routes by flying to Amsterdam Schiphol Airport or from various railway stations.

Last but not least, this book tells you everything about cycling in The Netherlands that you ever needed to know, which is handy as most of this information is usually only available in Dutch. Personally, I hope cycling in The Netherlands will bring you just as much joy as I have experienced myself since my childhood.

Eric van der Horst

Dutch cycling culture

In The Netherlands the bicycle is a natural means of transport. Cycling is so natural to most Dutch people that they just don't understand the excitement of international visitors about the Dutch cycling way of life. Dutch people grow up and live in a society ruled by bikes. They find it hard to imagine living in a world with a road network fully ruled by cars and don't realise how special the situation in their country is.

So what created this unique position of The Netherlands in the western world? As anywhere else in the 1950s and 1960s, motorised traffic grew rapidly in The Netherlands and roads started to get clogged up. But here is the thing: whilst in other countries nearly every individual made the transfer from bicycle to car, people in The Netherlands kept cycling as well.

With distances between places being small and the flat nature of the country, the bike was still a good alternative to the car and

remained popular. This caused a public demand by both drivers and cyclists to upgrade roads for both driving and cycling. Cycle paths and wide cycle lanes along main roads became standard features in Dutch infrastructure, as is designated signage for both drivers and cyclists.

For roads without adjusted infrastructure, there was still a call to protect cyclists further. With most drivers cycling themselves as well, it was easy to pass legislation recognising the vulnerable position of cyclists amongst motorised traffic. Drivers were made automatically liable for damage in accidents where cyclists were involved – a unique law making drivers continuously aware of cyclists.

Today, the Dutch keep building cycle paths, even along roads where there is hardly any motorised traffic. There are also thousands of miles of cycle paths away from roads (crossing nature reserves and farmland) built entirely for recreational purposes. On top of that you'll find Dutch on-road cycling extremely relaxing as well. Where there is no cycle path you'll find roads redesigned to keep cyclists going and to slow motorists down effectively. This is indeed a cyclist's paradise!

On the other hand, don't make the mistake of driving in The Netherlands. This is a transport nation, taking goods all over Europe. Main roads are heavily congested and the total length of all traffic jams in this small country is a popular topic on radio and TV (easily exceeding 180 miles in rush hour). With parking fees up to 30 Euros per hour in city centres, Dutch people like to avoid taking the car if they can. Going by bicycle is often quicker and cheaper at all times. If a destination is less than a 30-minute bike ride away, most Dutch people will cycle!

This makes Dutch people extremely skilled cyclists. People take not only their shopping on their bikes, but also their pets and children, even babies. Even women who are eight months pregnant still ride bikes. Normal life for a Dutch person: cycling for shopping, cycling to work, cycling to school, cycling to the pub. Simple!

Here is another interesting fact. There are more bikes than people in The Netherlands. A proper Dutch person owns three bicycles. Bike no. 1 is an unattractive-looking 'wreck', only to be used for rides to the train station. As it is normally parked there over a longer period of time in public space, the risk of bike theft (despite the bike's unattractiveness) is high. So, this bike comes with a decent lock, not only outweighing the bike itself in weight but also in value. This is the only way the owner can be sure to keep the ownership of the bike.

A popular alternative for this 'bike no. 1' is a folding bike, to be carried on trains for free during rush hours.

Bike no. 2 is a sturdy hybrid bicycle for shopping and other 'practical' day-to-day use. A pannier rack is essential, as are mudguards and dynamo lighting.

Bike no. 3 is the touring bike, to be kept in spotless condition, only allowed out of the garage on sunny days. This can be a racing bike or mountain bike, but also another sturdy hybrid bike with pannier rack, solely used for touring.

This is a very fashionable way to ride young children around town.

Summary of the main circular route

The main route is a 340 km circular route in central Netherlands, which could take up to 14 days to complete when cycling at a very easy pace. A main feature is the excellent tarmac cycling highway through the sand dune reserves of the Dutch coast, providing continuous direct access to Holland's sandy beaches. Starting from Hook of Holland you cycle via the city of The Hague. With the medieval seat of the Dutch government, the International Court and some world-class museums, it is worth spending a night here. There is also Madurodam, a miniature city with all the well-known buildings of The Netherlands in 1:25 scale. Beyond The Hague you can visit Duinrell theme park with the Tiki pool, Europe's largest covered waterslide paradise; don't forget to bring your swimming costume! The seaside towns of Katwijk and Noordwijk with their great beaches offer more swimming options. If you visit during April or May you should leave the coastal route for an additional ride through Holland's bulb fields; don't miss out on the famous Keukenhof Gardens!

Haarlem marks the end of the coastal route. This is a lovely old city with a medieval town square and scenic canals; much more quiet than those in busy Amsterdam and therefore much more enjoyable!

The coastal traffic-free cycle route takes you through various sand dune reserves.

Beyond Haarlem you pass the statue of the legendary (fictitious) boy, Hans Brinker, who put his finger in a Dutch dyke to prevent the land from flooding.

A bike ride in Holland wouldn't be complete without some serious windmill spotting and halfway between Haarlem and Amsterdam there is a great opportunity at the Zaanse Schans windmill reserve. Via Twiske Nature Reserve you'll reach the Dutch capital, Amsterdam.

Whether it is a visit to the Van Gogh Museum or Anne Frank House, a canal-boat tour or a walk through the infamous Red Light District, Amsterdam has it all. You might like to leave your bike at your accommodation, as city-centre cycling can be hectic. A pleasant circular bike route is included for those who would like to explore beyond the city's historic canal circle. This route takes you from the Central Station along the scenic Amstel River to popular green spaces like Amsterdamse Bos and Vondelpark.

De Haar Castle near Utrecht.

You'll see some fine architecture in quiet 18th- and 19th-century districts before returning to the Central Station via the city's best kept secret: the "Jordaan" area.

The main circular route continues along the busy Amsterdam-Rhine Canal where barges set off on their long journeys along the Rhine. This route takes you away from the city without having to cycle in any traffic.

The ride to the next city, Utrecht, gets its character from the sleepy Vecht River. This is where the merchants of the Dutch Golden Age built their country mansions and estates. There are plenty of opportunities for breaks on the way, especially at the original Dutch "Brooklyn Bridge". The Vecht River ends in the city of Utrecht, where its scenic "Old Canal" and one of Europe's tallest medieval church towers mix with countless shopping opportunities.

From Utrecht you cycle into Holland's Green Heart, a farmland belt of peace and quiet. Spend some time at the majestic De Haar Castle or the old Oudewater Witch Weighing

Table, before making your way to famous Gouda with its triangular Market Square. Don't miss the Gouda cheese farms en-route; these provide a unique opportunity to buy authentic Gouda cheese!

Heading back to the Dutch coast you'll cycle across Holland's lowest lands (22 ft below sea level) and you'll visit another famous Dutch town, Delft. This scenic old town full of Delftware is the last stop before completing the full circle. The last stretch between Delft and Hook of Holland takes you across a city of glass, an area of greenhouses where the Dutch produce their famous flowers for worldwide export 365 days a year.

Summary of additional routes

The guide contains three additional routes: one heading north from Amsterdam (80 km), one heading east from Maarssen (110 km) and one starting at the south western end of the country in Vlissingen, heading back to Hook of Holland (120 km). All additional routes connect with the main circular route and you'll have to take your bike on the train to either travel back or away from the main route. Route directions are chosen with the prevailing wind directions in mind.

The northern route takes you along the eastern shores of the North-Holland peninsula. These sheltered shores were tidal until 1932 when a dam at the northern tip of the peninsula was built to close off the Zuiderzee bay from the North Sea. This dam transformed this wide stretch of water in the centre of The Netherlands into a vast fresh-water lake, now named IJsselmeer. The ride offers plenty of views across the lake, taking in some classic Dutch horizons along the way. It is worth taking a break at the historic fishing harbours of Marken and Volendam before heading for pretty Edam. Despite being known worldwide for its cheeses, this small town is a haven of peace and quiet, with canals lining the streets.

From Edam the route continues northbound for Hoorn and Enkhuizen. These are both historic ports of the Dutch East India Trading Company, with fine medieval scenery as a matter of course. Enkhuizen also houses the Zuiderzee Museum, an open-air museum where traditional buildings from all around the former Zuiderzee coast have been relocated and restored – a great day out!

Most riders will take the train back to Amsterdam from Enkhuizen, but for those who are keen to do some serious mileage there is a real challenge to take on from Enkhuizen.

Volendam Harbour on the IJsselmeer coast (northern route).

The 30 km Enkhuizen-Lelystad dam ("Houtribdijk") across the IJsselmeer is the ultimate Dutch dyke ride with 20 miles of straight stretch exposed to the elements. Most of the cycle path on the dam is away from the main carriageway (which is on the other side of the dyke ridge). This means you'll be out there on your own most of the way, cycling within metres from the waves. This can be a fantastic experience during fine weather, but a bit of a killer if the wind is blowing from the wrong direction!

At the other end you can either board the train for Amsterdam in Lelystad or extend the ride into a full circle back to Amsterdam. Flevoland is an area only reclaimed from the sea in the 1950s and 1960s, offering great open vistas. Distances between places are long and there is not much to see and do, except the cycling itself. Even experienced riders should check wind directions first!

The eastern route in this guide is much more sheltered. This route takes you from Maarssen near Utrecht across forests and moorlands, offering a completely different experience of The Netherlands. Most of this "Utrecht Ridge" was recently designated as a National Park, with even some (modest) hills to take in! Make sure to have a pancake in one of the charming pancake restaurants on the way, as this is a traditional Dutch treat.

Traffic-free cycling in Utrecht Ridge National Park (eastern route)

The town of Amerongen marks the end of the forest ride. From here you take a ferry across one of the Rhine arms into the Betuwe, the predominant fruit-producing area of The Netherlands. This area was involved in a lot of military action during WWII. The Dutch army resisted the German invasion in 1940 for three days at the Grebbeberg, and in the city of Nijmegen you can look out over the old river bridge, taken by allied troops led by British army commander Montgomery in Operation Market Garden in 1944.

From Nijmegen it is a pleasant forested and even hilly circular ride to the National Liberation Museum, the place to check up on Operation Market Garden and the impact on the Dutch of the liberation from Nazi occupation. The route terminates in Nijmegen, the oldest city of The Netherlands, dating back from the Roman era. Take the train to Utrecht or Breukelen to rejoin the main route.

The southern route offers great coastal cycling, crossing wide estuaries via the most impressive flood barriers of the world. All barriers carry excellent cycle paths, separated from the main roads. This spectacular route also contains significant fine riding in sand dune reserves and forests, and with plenty of beach access.

Take the train to Vlissingen ("Flushing" in English), from where you follow a cycle route via a narrow coastal strip of sand dunes and forests. Small seaside resorts like Zoutelande and Domburg have a pleasant feel and you'll cycle via Westkapelle, The Netherlands' west cape.

Then you reach a series of huge barrier dams, together known as the "Delta Plan", a construction project which took over 40 years. The Delta Plan was initiated after the notorious 1953 floods when more than 1,800 people in the south-west of The Netherlands drowned.

The 1986 flood barrier in the Oosterschelde estuary will really blow your mind. It is the

The Oosterschelde flood barrier.

most expensive flood barrier ever built in the world and is about 6 miles long, with three series of floodgates over a total length of 2 miles. The barrier is a result of heated debates in the 1970s when environmental campaigners teamed up with the local seafood industry against the Delta Plan proposals to lock off the Oosterschelde estuary from the North Sea. The wide cycle path across the barrier is one of the most spectacular rides in The Netherlands, providing you have good weather.

The former island of Schouwen offers fine sand dune cycling with wide beaches, not to mention a medieval drowned village with

only the old church tower still standing on the sea defences.

The next estuary crossings take you to the former isles of Goeree and Voorne. Goedereede has an old scenic harbour, now completely located inland. Another significant town is Brielle, well known for its revolt against Spanish rule in the 1500s, sparking an 80-year-long Dutch war of independence. You rejoin the main circular route at Rotterdam Europoort via the link from the Hull ferry terminal to Hook of Holland (section 2, see page 40).

Planning your holiday

There are two main things to consider whilst planning your cycling holiday. In the first place you want to decide how to travel to The Netherlands, and in the second place you have to take the decision of whether to use your own bike or to rent a bike on arrival.

If you travel by ferry from the UK to The Netherlands, seriously consider leaving your car in a back street near the UK ferry terminal (or travel by train and/or cycle to the ferry). Travelling as a pedestrian on a ferry (with or without bike) is easy and much cheaper than bringing a car. As you are embarking on a cycling holiday you need to travel light anyway. If you prepare this well (see also gear and equipment), you can start cycling straight away once the ferry arrives in The Netherlands.

All ferry crossings between the UK and The Netherlands have long sailing times (the quickest being Harwich-Hook of Holland, taking six hours). Night crossings are most convenient, as you will travel while you sleep.

Some day crossings also operate. The earlier you book, the better the rates. You have the choice of three different routes, all serving various geographical parts of the UK.

Southern England, South Wales and South Midlands:
Harwich – Hook of Holland
Operated by Stenaline (www.stenaline.com)

North Wales, North Midlands and Lancashire/Yorkshire:
Hull – Rotterdam Europoort
Operated by P&O Ferries (www.poferries.com)

Northern England and Scotland:
Newcastle – Amsterdam IJmuiden
Operated by DFDS Seaways
(www.dfdsseaways.co.uk)

Travelling by bicycle on an overnight ferry.

All three Dutch ports are connected to the circular route in this guidebook. If you bring your own bike, you can immediately start cycling! Note: only Hook of Holland has a railway station (Hoek van Holland-Haven) and bike rental close to the ferry terminal. The bike rental in Hook of Holland is a five-minute walk away from the terminal, located on the main street in Hook's town centre:

Hook of Holland bike rental.

Profile Kees van den Burg
Prins Hendrikstraat 235/241
3151 AJ Hoek van Holland
+ 31 174 382318
Email: profilekees-vanden-burg@planet.nl
www.profilekeesvandenburg.nl/verhuur

If you arrive at the Rotterdam Europoort terminal as a pedestrian and you want to rent a bike, it is best to use the bike rental in Hook of Holland. To get there you'll need to travel by coach to Rotterdam Central Station, from where you can take the train to station Hoek van Holland-Haven. This journey can take up to 90 minutes. Note: you'll need to pre-book the coach service from the ferry terminal to Rotterdam Central Station via P&O (operated by Eurolines).

If you arrive at the IJmuiden terminal as a pedestrian and you want to rent a bike, it is best to use a bike rental in Haarlem. Walk 10 minutes from the ferry terminal to the Zwaanstraat bus stop and catch bus 75. This service runs approximately twice per hour and brings you to Haarlem Central Station in about 30 minutes. From there it is a five-minute walk to the bike rental below. Join the route of the guidebook at Haarlem's central square, "Grote Markt", literally around the corner.

Rent a Bike Haarlem (De fietsfanaat)
Parklaan 47
2011 KR Haarlem
+ 31 23 5421195
Email: info@rentabikehaarlem.nl
www.rentabikehaarlem.nl

The fleet of Dutch bike rentals mostly consists of Dutch-style city bikes or hybrids with high-up handlebars, mudguards and luggage rack. Try to avoid renting a bike without any gears and/or coaster brakes (braking by pedalling backwards). These bikes are not suitable for the longer journeys you want to embark on. When collecting the bike you should do a test ride around the block to ensure you are completely happy. Make sure you also get a good lock (with key) and a repair kit with pump!

Expect to pay up to €15 per bike per day, although you might get a discount for long-term hire. You will be required to leave some kind of deposit, like a bank card, credit card or passport, at the rental site whilst you are away with the bike. Note; credit cards can rarely be used for the actual payment itself.

Of course, there are more places where you can rent a bike. Over 100 railway stations have a bike rental in or next to the railway station. In scenic areas there are also various independent rentals. The magic word to look out for is "fietsverhuur" ("bike rental" in Dutch). Rental fleet, fees and deposits will be much the same everywhere.

If you choose to fly to The Netherlands via Amsterdam Schiphol Airport, we recommend the following bike hire:

Bike City Rental Amsterdam
Bloemgracht 68-70
1015 TL Amsterdam
+ 31 20 6263721
www.bikecity.nl

To get there, travel by train to Amsterdam Central Station and take either tram 13 or 17 to the "Westermarkt" stop (this is also the Anne Frank House stop). From here it is a five-minute walk to the rental. Start cycling by using the Amsterdam City Ride of this guidebook, joining via the Prinsengracht at the Anne Frank House (see page 79).

Of course you can also bring your own bike on a plane, but this procedure is quite advanced. In the first place you'll have to find an airline happy to transport your bike at a reasonable rate. Most airlines will require you to pack your bike in a carton box or plastic bag. You'll need to turn the handlebars and take off the pedals and the front wheel. This is really only worth doing for long-haul flights – for example, if you wish to visit The Netherlands from America, Australia or Israel. For your flight home, it is good to know bike boxes are for sale at Amsterdam Schiphol Airport for around €15. Take the bike on the train between the airport and Amsterdam Central Station and start and finish our routes from there. Luggage storage in secure lockers is available at Central Station for 72 hours, at Schiphol Airport for 7 days, costing €5 - €10 per day.

Gear and equipment

The routes in this book take you around the country. This means you will only occasionally spend the night in the same place twice. You'll have to carry your own luggage on your bike whilst travelling from A to B. As riding with a bag on your back is uncomfortable, makes you sweat and wears your back out after a while, it makes sense to adapt your bike slightly to carry luggage on the bike.

It doesn't matter what kind of bike you ride, but you should get a rack fixed above the rear wheel, so you can carry at least two pannier bags on the back. Racks used to be fitted standard to bikes (and still are in The Netherlands), but manufacturers often leave them off these days, as it makes bikes cheaper to buy. A rack only costs between £20 and £30 (a proper bike shop will put the rack on your bike without extra charge), and will bring lots of convenience in the long term. Make sure you also get some elastics, so you can also carry a small bag, rucksack or coat on top of the rack. Whilst you are at it, you also might

like to get some mudguards and a chain cover fitted to your bike. These are all features bicycle manufacturers don't include these days to save costs, but they have their good use and are still very much standard in The Netherlands.

A set of two pannier bags will enable you to carry luggage for a cycling holiday up to two weeks, providing you stay at indoor accommodation and have the opportunity to do some laundry halfway. Outdoor panniers are the best and the German manufacturer, Ortlieb, sets the standard for this kind of bag. Ortlieb bags are guaranteed waterproof and last a lifetime. With Ortlieb being on the pricey side, it is worthwhile having a look at similar products on the market. Bear in mind that the cheaper you go, the more likely it is that the bag or fittings will be damaged or broken with regular use.

Me – Eric van der Horst – ready for a camping tour at a Dutch railway station. I have been riding this Dutch hybrid bike for many years on long journeys in various countries. For B&B touring you'll only need the two side (pannier) bags at the back.

Of course, there are also ordinary panniers on the market, more intended for occasional shopping. These bags are cheaper and have less volume available to fill. Be prepared to pack all your goods in plastic bags within these panniers, as they might not be waterproof. Have a browse and make sure you purchase panniers that fit your budget and meet the requirements for not only your holiday in The Netherlands, but also for future use.

If you intend to do some camping on your cycling holiday you will generally need another set of panniers to fit everything in. Front panniers are different to rear panniers and need a special front rack in order to be carried.

On a cycling holiday with indoor accommodation only you should be able to fit the following in your panniers:

- 2 sets of clothes to be used for cycling during the day, including shirt, jumper and trousers/shorts
- 1 easy set of clothes to wear at night (pyjamas, etc)
- 1 nice set of clothes (for non-cycling related travelling and going out; don't use this set for sweaty activities!)
- More than a sufficient amount of socks and underwear

- Proper waterproofs (coat and trousers), which can withstand cold winds and with a breathable layer inside
- Light outfit for hot weather, including sun cap
- Small bag for toiletries
- Small bicycle repair kit

Your bicycle repair kit should contain an easy-to-use combination tool with various functions (like spanners and screwdrivers). If this tool doesn't contain a spanner that enables you to take off a wheel, bring a spanner that can. Of course, you also bring a pump and a spare tube with some tyre lifters. If you want to be able to fix punctures yourself, buy patches that don't need glue (like Super Patch). If you buy a new spare tube in The Netherlands, make sure the tube valve is compatible with your pump.

Camping by bike is fun, but requires a full set of pannier bags (back and front), not recommended for novice cyclists. Get some experience on a B&B tour first!

With a basic repair kit like this you will be able to fix punctures and do most emergency adjustments to brakes and gears.

You should not be afraid of getting into trouble with your bike. If you make sure your bicycle is in good condition before starting your holiday, it is very unlikely you'll run into trouble. A proper bike check beforehand makes for happy cycling:

- Check air pressure of tyres and ensure there is plenty of tread left on the tyres; if the thread is worn or when you can see deep holes or rips in the rubber, get a new tyre!

- Carefully check the area around the valve; is the tube still properly in place or is it sliding (valve hanging diagonally)? Get a new tube if the valve area is damaged!

- Check both the front and the rear brakes; are all cables working properly and are the brake pads in a good state?

- Check if all elements of the bike are properly fitted; nuts and bolts need to be tightened up properly!

- Check the seat height – when sitting on the saddle you should be on tiptoes – also, is the seat comfortable enough for a cycling holiday? If not, treat yourself to a nice soft seat; they are not expensive these days and life is too short to cycle on a bike with a rock-hard saddle!

If you are nervous about doing these checks yourself, take the bike to a repair shop for a check-up. Explain that you are going on a cycling holiday soon to ensure the mechanic will do a job up to the task ahead!

It is recommended that (at least) one person in your party gets a bike computer fitted. This kind of computer, showing speed and mileage, enables you to follow the route instructions in this guidebook easily. Note: you'll have to switch the settings to kilometres, as this is the standard being used in The Netherlands. Bike computers come in all price ranges but the simplest ones will be adequate. Also, please be reassured that you don't need outdoor GPS equipment to cycle this guidebook's routes. Do get a waterproof map holder for on the handlebars though. The format of this guidebook is especially designed to fit in such holders.

Another must is a proper lock on your bike. The down side of a prominent cycling culture is bike theft and all bicycles left unattended are at risk of being stolen in The Netherlands. Always lock your bicycle to a secure object like a bike rack or lamp post, even when you are away from your bike for only a minute. In busy cities like The Hague, Amsterdam or Utrecht, even a good lock doesn't provide enough protection. In these places you should make use of guarded bike parking. You'll find them at railway stations and at central locations in the main cities. When walking your bike in busy places, always hold on firmly to the handlebars of your bike and be aware of your surroundings. The ferry landings at Amsterdam Central Station are notorious for thieves snatching bikes out of people's hands!

The final thing you should think about when preparing for your holiday is whether you are going to use a cycling helmet or not. If you do, it is important to bring your own, as the use of helmets (and also high-visibility vests) is largely unknown in The Netherlands. If you intend to rent bikes, you won't be able to hire helmets as well. Helmets are for sale in Dutch bike shops, but don't expect much choice. The stock available mostly caters for racing cyclists.

Without getting too much into the cycle helmet debate, it is good to read the following statement of the European Cyclist's Federation (ECF), also endorsed by the British Cyclists' Touring Club (CTC):

"ECF is not opposed to the wearing of bicycle helmets, but firmly believes that this should be a decision for each individual cyclist. The countries with the highest level of cycle use and the lowest risks per kilometre cycled (read: "The Netherlands") have chosen to create safer road conditions rather than promote the wearing of helmets."

Regarding the weather, you can best visit The Netherlands from May to September. April is only worthwhile if you want to see the blooming tulip fields (blooming until mid-May). The first week of May, the last weeks of July and the first weeks of August are busy with holidaymakers, so make reservations well in advance for these periods.

Dutch traffic rules

Cyclists in the Netherlands are fully accepted as road users by all traffic participants. You'll find most Dutch drivers are extremely generous to cyclists, but don't take this for granted. Cyclists not obeying traffic rules are a growing annoyance to drivers and might put the special Dutch cyclist's liability law at risk. To be a responsible cyclist in The Netherlands you should read this chapter, as Dutch traffic rules can be considerably different at some points.

Cycling on the right-hand side
In continental Europe you keep right on the roads, so you cycle on the right-hand side, whether you are on a road or on a cycle path. Where there are cycle paths on both sides of a main road, you should be on the path on the right-hand side of the road, unless it is a two-way cycle path (with lines in the middle of the path).

If you are used to riding on the left, keeping right is a serious blow to all natural reflexes you normally use when participating in traffic.

Be extremely cautious when approaching and taking junctions! Work out for yourself where you are supposed to cycle before you make a move and keep reminding each other to cycle on the right, especially on quiet country lanes or paths.

Use of cycle paths and cycle lanes
If there is a cycle path adjacent to a main road, you must use the path. You will not only be honked at by drivers if you don't, but you can also be fined for cycling on a main carriageway. Most Dutch cycle paths are designed to keep going at reasonable speed without the need to slow down. You'll rarely find blind corners, very sharp curves or sudden endings. Only when the cycle path has a sign with the text "fietspad" (meaning "cycle path" in Dutch) is the use of the cycle path optional, so you can also use the main carriageway. In all other situations, where the cycle path has a sign with the white bicycle symbol on a blue background, you have to use the path.

Sign of a "must use" path.

Sign of an optional cycle path ("fietspad").

Also, there are some major roads where cycling is not allowed at all. In this situation, the "no cycling" sign will be clearly displayed (see below).

Regarding on-road cycle lanes, we recommend keeping within the lane as much as possible. Look over your shoulder first before you move out of a cycle lane and only if you really have to. If the lane is wide enough you can cycle two abreast as well.

In general, you can cycle two abreast at any time, providing there is enough space and you don't block the way for another traffic participant. Be always ready to cycle single file – for example, when an overtaking cyclist is using his/her bell or when a driver wants to overtake you. It might be appealing to cycle three abreast or more on some routes, but be aware this is not legal and you can be fined for doing so.

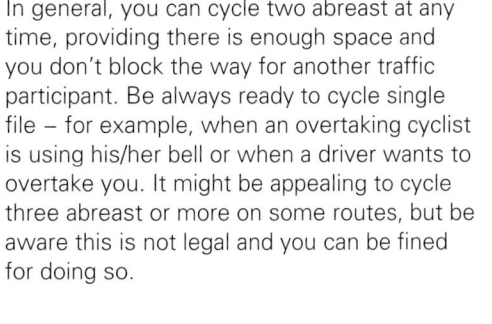

Typical on-road cycle lanes. Many Dutch roads have layouts with only one lane for motorised traffic and wide cycle lanes on both sides. This makes these roads less attractive for through-traffic and slows motorists down considerably. Dangerous overtaking of cyclists is further tackled by additional traffic signs (see above).

Pedestrians

If a path is marked as a cycle path, pedestrians are welcome to use the path as well, but cyclists have priority. It is completely acceptable to use your bell when overtaking pedestrians. They will normally make way for you immediately, so you don't have to slow down at all. Please do slow down when you are overtaking children or people with dogs that are not on a lead.

Watch out for footpaths not dedicated for cycling. As soon as you see a sign displaying the international footpath symbol (man walking with child) or a sign mentioning the word "voetpad" ("footpath" in Dutch), you should dismount and walk. Also, watch out for common signs with the text "verboden te fietsen", which means "no cycling" in Dutch. When walking yourself, keep in mind that walking on a cycle path is not accepted if there is an adjacent footpath.

Priority issues – crossings

On some cycle-path crossings you have priority over the traffic on the road you are crossing; on others you don't. Look out for the white triangle "give way" signs on the tarmac/pavement, or for a white triangle sign with red lining. This will indicate who goes first.

In the examples above you have to give way. In the picture on the right, there are not only white triangles on the tarmac, but also a give way sign. In this picture you have to give way three times:
1. To pedestrians using the zebra crossing on the cycle path
2. To cyclists on the cycle path of the other road
3. To traffic on the main carriageway of the other road

In the two pictures above you have right of way when crossing the main carriageway. This is indicated by the white triangle markings on the main carriageway.

In the left-hand picture you have to give way before crossing (note the white triangles on the tarmac); in the right-hand picture you have right of way when crossing the road (note the white triangles on the main carriageway left of the cycle path crossing). Again, you only use these priority rules when the traffic lights are not working!

If you encounter traffic lights, the lights rule. However, various Dutch traffic lights get switched off during the quiet hours of the day, which can be confusing. In this situation, the amber lights will be flashing (as a warning for the junction) and the additional give way markings on the road surface indicate who has priority.

Priority issues – turning traffic

In most countries, traffic turning into side roads has to give way to traffic on the main road that goes straight on. In The Netherlands, this rule includes cyclists on cycle paths adjacent to main roads. This means you should not need to worry about turning traffic if you are on a cycle path.

Yes, the turning driver in the picture above will definitely wait for you if you were on this cycle path. Also, in the middle picture, you have right of way above turning traffic. Why? This cycle path is actually situated on a speed bump. The bump indicates to drivers that they have to give way!

There are some busier side roads, though, where cyclists on cycle paths have to give way to turning traffic. In this situation you'll always find clear "give way" signs at the junction and clear markings on the cycle path's surface.

Priority issues – junctions without priority markings

In The Netherlands there are also many "equal junctions", meaning that traffic on one road doesn't have priority over traffic on the other road. You can recognise these junctions easily, as they don't show any priority signs or markings at all. In these situations, traffic from the right has priority at all times! **This rule also includes T-junctions!** So if you are cycling on a road without priority markings that goes straight on at a T-junction and there is a road feeding into this road from the right, all traffic on that road has priority above you!

*Note the two roads coming from the right, just beyond the bus stop. In both situations the "equal junctions" rule applies, so **traffic from the right goes first**!*

Another example: even though the road straight on 'feels' like a main road, traffic on the road from the right goes first! Note the road lining stops to confirm this.

For all priority issues it is good to stick to the "golden rule": before using a priority right you should establish eye contact with the other traffic participant to check that you have been noticed. If you are not sure about your priority right or you get the impression the other traffic participant is not going to wait for you, stop!

One-way streets

Most one-way streets in The Netherlands have an exemption contra flow for cyclists, with or without an actual contra flow cycling lane painted on the surface. Look for the international "no entry" sign at the beginning of the one-way street to check if this exemption exists. Under the red sign with the white line you'll see an additional white sign with the picture of a bicycle with the Dutch text "uitgezonderd", meaning "except". Only if there is no additional sign showing the exemption does the "no entry" sign also apply to cyclists.

Cyclists can ignore the traffic sign if the "uitgezonderd" sign is shown as well. There are also "uitgezonderd" signs in combination with other signs, like for dead-end roads that are not a dead end for cyclists!

Hazards for cyclists in The Netherlands

Although cyclists are generally very safe in The Netherlands, there are some hazards that can be regarded as typically Dutch. The biggest problem, despite all the cycling infrastructure, is the legal use of mopeds, scooters and small cars (for use by the disabled) on most cycle paths. These vehicles should obey a 45 km/h (30 mph) speed limit, but some people (especially youngsters) ride their mopeds too fast. This causes nuisance amongst cyclists, especially in urban zones. Always keep a straight line and do not suddenly change direction without a clear signal when you hear or see a motorised vehicle approaching on a cycle path.

Tram tracks are another thing of which to be aware. The Hague and Amsterdam have extensive tram networks and it is inevitable that you'll have to cross some tram tracks. Go straight across and never diagonally!

If you have to cross a railway level crossing, take extreme care. After a train has passed you must wait until all lights and warning sounds are completely switched off (even if the barriers are opening again). These systems operate automatically and the barriers might close again for a train approaching from the other direction!

In town centres you have to be on your guard for bollards that sink and rise from below the road surface. You find them on designated bus routes and in shopping streets. Never cycle over a sunken bollard as it can rise at any time! Further, on some popular cycle paths you might find speed bumps. These are designed to slow racing cyclists down. Look out for signs warning for "drempels" or "verkeersdrempels" and slow down.

Last but not least, watch out for water! You might cycle right next to a deep ditch or canal, so stick to the tarmac.

Crossing tram tracks safely and waiting at a level crossing.

Dutch cycle route signage

Dutch signs with cycle route information form a world of their own and leave most international visitors confused and impressed at the same time. Cycling is more fun if you understand the various signage systems, so here we go!
To start, the general road signs with white lettering on a blue background mostly apply to motorised traffic only. At nearly every junction you'll find additional cycle route signs with red lettering on a white background.

White signs are for cyclists only.

Blue signs are mostly for motorised traffic.

These signs often show the distance in kilometres to a location and should always show the most direct route. These routes are often not the most scenic ones. If there is a nicer (but longer) alternative route to the same location, the sign will show this in green italic lettering. Once the name of a location appears on a sign, you can be pretty sure you'll be guided all the way to this destination. All signs also have a unique number on their base and detailed maps published by the Dutch AA (ANWB) will show this number – a great help if you want to know exactly where you are. The maps in this guidebook don't show the sign numbers.

In some places, especially nature reserves, you will also find so-called "paddestoelen" ("mushroom signs"). These are signs near to ground level and in the shape of a mushroom. Lettering is in a small font, so you have to slow down to be able to read them. They have the same function as the regular signs at eye height and are also numbered. "Paddestoelen" are a remainder of an older signage system that was in use until the 1960s. They are kept for reasons of nostalgia and in some places even new ones are erected!

LF-signs is mostly in green, sometimes in red. All LF-routes have signage for both directions: one direction with the adjective "a", the other with adjective "b".

The classic "mushroom sign".

Another signage system besides the straightforward location signs is the so-called LF-network. This is a network of long-distance cycle routes, designed for leisure cycling, guiding you along pretty routes and places of interest. These routes are perfectly signposted and some of them cross borders into Belgium and Germany. The oldest LF-route is the North Sea Route LF 1, running between Bologne Sur Mer in France and Den Helder in The Netherlands. LF-routes don't normally take the shortest routes available. The lettering on

Signs for LF 2 (Amsterdam-Brussels) and LF 23 (Zuiderzeeroute), a popular circuit LF-route.

Recently, a new system has been introduced in addition to the LF-network. This is the "knooppunt"-network and consists of a numbering system for junctions rather than routes. In between these numbered junctions you'll only find signs with the number of the next junction you are heading for. Distances between junctions vary from 1 to 6 miles. To make the system work, you'll find a sign with a map of the area at every junction of the network, showing you the other numbered "junctions" nearby. This system is being introduced region by region. Important lingo: "knooppunt" = "junction"; "u nadert knooppunt ..." = "you are approaching junction..."

At every "knooppunt" you should find a sign with a detailed map so you can decide on the spot where to head next. Note: this is the map of junction 86.

The "knooppunt"-network is slowly replacing a system of hexagonal scenic cycle route signs. These routes are perfectly signed themed circuit routes, varying in distance from 10 to 30 miles. Some of these signed routes might survive, as locals are very attached to them, if only for their names. What about the "smugglers route" on the border with Belgium and The Netherlands, or the "small ferries route", including various ferry crossings over tiny canals ...

Hexagonal themed route sign, very popular in Belgium too and even named after a famous cyclist!

Information about signed routes is available from tourist offices. The Dutch AA (ANWB) is the main publisher of route guides, but as these are only available in Dutch or German, you will be limited to using the maps. The routes in this guidebook offer a combination of all available routes and use the best route sections available.

Sign of the "knooppunt"-network. This is junction "knooppunt" 9. To get to junction 6 you go straight on, to get to junction 10, turn right.

Accommodation

Accommodation can be expensive. Hotels are pricey and Dutch B&Bs mostly cater for up-market customers. To keep the costs down, there are two good alternatives.

The first alternative is staying in hostels. YHA-hostels in The Netherlands have been renamed "Stay Okay" and have been extensively refurbished in recent years. They cater not only for younger people but also for families and anyone who wants to save on accommodation expenses. A YHA-membership is not required, but if you intend staying multiple nights it might be worthwhile becoming a member, as members get discounts. On the main circular route you'll find hostels in The Hague, Noordwijk, Haarlem and Amsterdam. The eastern route is served by hostels in Soest and Elst. On the southern route you can stay in the Domburg hostel. See also www.stayokay.nl

Despite the presence of the Stay Okay hostels there are still some considerable gaps in the routes of this guide without budget accommodation. That is why you should look into the following alternative. This is the "Vrienden op de Fiets" ("Friends on the Bike") charity with a database of about 3,700 places to stay in The Netherlands and Belgium, providing you travel by bicycle or foot and become a member.

This is a network of cyclists who like to host other cyclists and offer one night's accommodation in their private homes. Charges don't exceed € 18.50 per person per night and the membership fee is only € 9 for a family. This gives you the opportunity to meet other bike-minded people and also provides a great insight into Dutch culture. Sign up via www.vriendenopdefiets.nl. Do this well in advance of your holiday as the joining process might take up to six weeks.

Camping is of course another way to save on accommodation expenses. There are plenty of campsites in The Netherlands, varying in size and levels of luxury. Options in built-up areas can be limited, so really plan ahead and make reservations if possible. Expect to pay up to € 10 per person or € 15 per pitch per night.

Both accommodation and campsite suggestions are listed in the back of this guidebook and also include some more expensive hotels and B&Bs. Note: addresses of the "Friends on the Bike" charity are not included – you need to become a member to get their address book. The accommodation list refers back to the map pages on which the facility is marked with a corresponding letter. There is no need to worry if you have to travel slightly away from the cycle route of this guidebook to get to a facility. There is good cycling infrastructure everywhere, so you won't end up cycling in busy, fast-moving traffic.

Travelling by train

Train tickets in The Netherlands are generally cheap. There is no need to buy pre-booked tickets, as these are the same price as tickets bought on the day. Timetables can be found on big display signs at stations and via www.ns.nl.

Taking bicycles on Dutch trains.

Dutch Railways (Nederlandse Spoorwegen) only carry folded bikes for free. For any other bike you'll have to pay € 6 per bike. This "dagkaart fiets" (bicycle day ticket) is valid for one day and has unlimited mileage, so only a good deal if you travel long-distance. Most trains have designated spaces for bikes, but note that you can't use these on weekdays between 6.30-9.00 am, and 4.30-6.00 pm. At weekends and during July and August, you can take a bike on the train at any time. Taking the train is a great way to move quickly across the country to the route of your choice.

General travel information

As a traveller it is always important to be aware of local customs, especially if it affects the traveller directly. Here are some aspects of Dutch society that might be entirely different to where you come from.

In the first place you need to know that credit cards are not widely accepted for payments. Most shops and accommodation only accept payments by Dutch bank card ("pinnen") or cash ("contant"). This means the international visitor will end up paying cash most of the time. Fortunately, ATMs ("geldautomaat") are widespread, so it is easy to get cash out with a card carrying the Cirrus, Maestro, Visa or Mastercard logo. As there will be transaction and exchange-rate charges it is advisable to take out cash in bigger chunks. Separate this cash out over various safe spaces; never keep it all in your main wallet!

Secondly you have to know that opening times of most Dutch shops are limited from 9 am to 5 pm or 6 pm on weekdays and Saturdays. Monday mornings are notorious for shops not opening until midday. "Shopping nights" are either on Thursdays or Fridays (shops open until 9 pm).

Some supermarkets are licensed to be open until 8 pm. Sunday shopping is irregular, limited to once or twice a month, mostly in tourist places. Dutch supermarkets are generally small and 24-hour superstores and/or corner shops are largely unknown.

Also, don't be surprised if you receive some poor customer service at some stage of your holiday. Unless you are shopping in an international environment you'll find that Dutch shopkeepers are not interested in their customers most of the time. Paying cash you'll also notice that in most shops you will get change in rounded figures, so up or down to the very next 5 Euro Cent. Some shops even refuse to take 1 and 2 Euro Cent coins, despite it being legal tender. The Dutch themselves are completely accustomed to this poor standard of customer service.

Public toilets are another annoyance whilst travelling in The Netherlands. These hardly exist and if you can find one, expect to pay up to a euro to visit the toilet. Don't expect much of these facilities, despite the charge. Public places like bars and restaurants are not keen to offer toilet facilities to non-customers, either. In big department stores you end up paying even as a customer. The prying eyes of staff don't let you be until you put the required coins down onto the designated saucer at the exit!

Food: Dutch specialities

This guidebook mostly limits itself to cycling issues, and the facilities and attractions you'll find directly on the cycling routes. If you want to extend your visit to The Netherlands for multiple days beyond the cycling it might be worth buying a general guidebook, like Lonely Planet or Rough Guide. These books have extensive sections about fine dining, nightlife and so on. However, at this stage we'd like to draw your attention to some simple typically Dutch delights, hardly mentioned by the big guides and beyond the easy cheese and beer. Here we go!

Dutch bakeries: With plenty of choice of fresh bread these are worth repeated visits. Don't forget to have a slice of apple pie ("appeltaart") or cherry pie ("kersenvlaai") in a café as well!

Dutch fruit pies of high quality can also be bought at the "Multivlaai" chain.

Chocolate sprinkles: The Dutch are very bread-orientated for every meal. Especially for breakfast the Dutch like to "decorate" their sandwiches with margarine and sprinkles; look out for "hagelslag" and "vlokken" on the shelves.

Pancakes: Only a "pannenkoekenrestaurant" provides the full Dutch pancake experience. Dutch pancakes are the size of pizzas and beyond the main choice between savoury and sweet there are dozens of topping options. These restaurants cater for both lunch and dinner.

Take away: The Dutch "snackbar" has chips ("patat") on its main menu, but watch out for the sauces! "Patat met" is chips with mayonnaise, "patatje pinda" is chips with peanut sauce, "patatje oorlog" is chips with ketchup, mayonnaise and onions. Meaty snacks are often on display in coin-operated boxes (self service).

Indonesian: The colonial era has left The Netherlands with a distinguished taste for Indonesian food. Try a "rijst tafel" (various rice dishes combined) in a proper restaurant!

Vegetarian: The Netherlands is very meat-orientated. It is hard to find tasty veggie meals, even in a restaurant.

Dairy: The Dutch love dairy. A special treat are their yoghurts and custards for desert; "dubbelvla" (a combination of vanilla and chocolate custard) is a favourite!

Tip for those who like dairy: some Dutch farms offer fresh (non-pasteurised) milk via self-service machines.

Language

The Netherlands is an easy country to get around as an international visitor. Most Dutch people speak English to a general level, but specific information in English (like this guidebook) can be very limited. You shouldn't have trouble finding your way and/or making yourself understood in most public places. To be able to understand a bit of the Dutch written language it is good to know that a lot of words are formed from a string of short words, together forming a very long word. For the meaning of some of the very common words present on Dutch roads (and beyond), have a look at the glossary on the next couple of pages. This will help you to read signs. Some other important words are also included in the list, but if you really want to know about Dutch language you should buy a general guidebook or a specific language book.

"Verboden toegang" means no trespassing.

Dutch	English	Dutch	English	Dutch	English
afgesloten	closed	eiland	island	kabel	cable
alstublieft	please	fiets	bicycle	kade	quay
andere richtingen	other directions	fietsen	to cycle	kerk	church
auto	car	fietser	cyclist	klein	small
baan	path, way	geen	no, none	laan	avenue
betalen	to pay	geld	money	langzaam	slow
binnen	inside, inner	geldautomaat	ATM/cash machine	markt	market
bloem	flower	gemeente	council	molen	windmill
boot	ship	gesloten	closed	nee	no
brug	bridge	goede middag	good afternoon	niet	no
buiten	outside, outer	goede morgen	good morning		
burg	fort	goedenavond	good evening		
contant	cash only	gracht	canal		
dag	day	groot	great, large		
dag	hello!	haven	harbour		
dank u	thank you	hoek	corner		
dicht	closed	hoi	hi		
dijk	dyke	huis	house		
doorgaand verkeer	through traffic	ja	yes		
drempel	speed bump	kaart	map		
dwars	transverse	kaartje	ticket		

nieuw	new	station	station
noord	north	steeg	alley
omleiding	diversion	straat	street
oost	east	tot ziens	bye!
open	open	trein	train
oud	old	veld	field
pad	path	veer	ferry (possibly pedestrian)
paard	horse	verboden te fietsen	no cycling
perron	platform	verkeer	traffic
plein	square	vliegveld	airport
pont	ferry (possibly pedestrian)	voetgangers	pedestrians
poort	gate	vracht	freight
schip	ship	wal	embankment
sloot	ditch	wc	toilet
slot	castle	weg	road
slot	lock (in a door or on a bike)	welkom	welcome
		west	west
sluis	lock (in a canal)	werk in uitvoering	road works
sluizen	locks (in a canal)	wijk	district/estate
snelweg	motorway, interstate	winkel	shop
spoor	railway, railway tracks	zuid	south

Section 1 (link): IJmuiden – Main Route (11 km)

Use this section if you travel to The Netherlands from Newcastle and are using your own bike(s). This link connects to the main route at Spaarndam (just north of Haarlem). If you need a rental bike you'll have to travel to Haarlem by bus and start the route there (see page 15).

Although advertised as Amsterdam by the ferry company, IJmuiden is an independent town, now absorbed by the Haarlem agglomeration. The history of IJmuiden only dates back to 1876 when a new shipping canal was dug across the Dutch sand dunes to provide inland Amsterdam with a direct sea link. To get to the Amsterdam docks, ships have to navigate through one of IJmuiden's massive sea locks. IJmuiden itself has limited docking facilities. The town with its towering steelworks nearby might feel a bit depressed, but you have to remember it is the nearby beach and sand dune nature reserves that are the focus for the locals.

The link takes you via IJmuiden's main shopping area to the village of Spaarndam. On the way you'll cycle through Driehuis and Santpoort, two Haarlem suburbs. As you'll need this link twice (also for the return journey), instructions for both directions of travel are provided. You'll find the connecting main route in Spaarndam on page 67.

The Dutch coast at IJmuiden.

From IJmuiden to Spaarndam:

0.0 **Cycle on right-hand side!**
From ferry →, reset computer at bend to left

0.5 1st rd ← (Magadantstr), 1st rd ←, 1st rd ↗ (uphill)

0.8 At jct → (Wilhelminakade)

1.0 At jct →, at rndabt ↖ (Kennemerlaan), poor 🚲!

2.2 At shopping street ← via 🚲 on left-hand side

2.5 2nd rd → (Velserduinweg)

3.0 Cross main rd via lhts, ← via 🚲 on right-hand side

4.3 After disused railway at rndabt → (to Crematorium)

4.8 4th rd → (to Crematorium)

5.3 1st "fietspad" ← (to KP 5)

6.1 Ep ↖, at T-jct → (to KP 5)

6.9 At jct ↖ (Middenduinweg), ↑ at railway and rndabt

7.7 1st rd → (Velserhooftlaan)

8.1 At jct ← (Wustelaan)

8.3 At rndabt ⬆ via 🚲, ↑ via tunnel (to Spaarndam)

11.3 Hans Brinker statue, end link

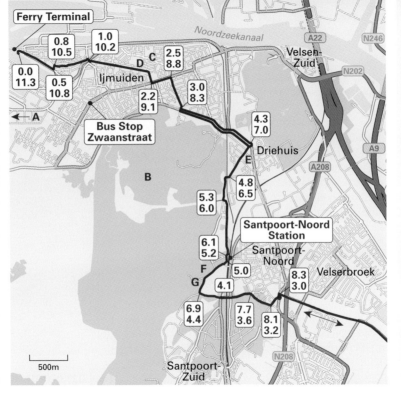

From Spaarndam to IJmuiden:

0.0 ← via rd on dyke ridge

0.4 ↑ via 🚲 on left-hand side

3.0 Ep ⬆ (Wustelaan)

3.2 2nd rd → (Velserhooftlaan)

3.6 1st rd ← (Middenduinenw)

4.1 After rndabt & railway ↑ via quiet rd (Middenduinenw)

4.4 ↗ (Duin en Kruidbergerw)

5.0 Before railway ← (to KP 4)

5.2 1st "fietspad" ↗ (to KP 4)

6.0 Ep → via rd (to KP 4)

6.5 After railway 1st rd ← (Driehuizerkerkw, to KP 4)

7.0 At rndabt ← via 🚲 on right-hand side (to IJmuiden), ↑

8.3 At lhts on main rd → (Velserduinweg), keep ↖

8.8 At shopping street ← via 🚲 on right-hand side

9.1 1st rd → (Marktplein, later Kennemerlaan), poor 🚲!

10.2 At rndabt ↗ via bridge, 1st rd ← (Wilhelminakade)

10.5 1st rd ↖ (walk bike down!)

10.8 At T-jct ↙, 2x at T-jct →

Section 2 (link): Europoort – Main Route (20 km)

Use this section if you travel to The Netherlands from Hull and are using your own bike(s). This link connects the Hull ferry terminal with the main route at Hook of Holland. If you arrive from Hull without bikes you'll need to travel to Hook of Holland by coach and train, see page 15. If you have cycled the Southern route you'll also need part of this link to travel either to Hook or the Hull terminal.

It is important to be mentally prepared for the sheer size of the Europoort Rotterdam docks. Rotterdam is Europe's biggest harbour, continuously expanding into the North Sea on newly reclaimed land, known as "Maasvlakte". Even in this surreal industrial landscape you'll find good cycle paths, but be prepared for some strong headwinds and stock up on provisions as there is not much out there until you get to Hook.

It will take approximately one hour of pedalling to reach the pedestrian ferry to Hook of Holland. This ferry is operated by Rotterdam public transport RET (www.ret.nl) and operates between Europoort (landing "Maasvlakte") and Hook. It runs daily (Mon-Fri every 30 mins until 8 pm, weekends every hour until 7 pm, € 3 single, bikes free); don't miss the last ferry from the "Maasvlakte" landing!

The ferry terminal at Hook of Holland marks the start of the main circular route for travellers on both the Harwich and Hull ferries. Those who travel on the Hull ferry have to add 90 minutes of travel time to get there (either by cycling or using public transport).

From Hull Terminal to Hook:

0.0 **Cycle on right-hand side!**
Reset computer at start
🚲 on right-hand side (see
🚲 sign "All directions")

0.5 After railway cross rd ↑,
then ← via 🚲 on right-
hand side of rd

2.1 1st 🚲 ← onto high bridge
(to Maasvlakte), keep going
↑ next to motorway

6.1 At T-jct → via 🚲 (to Hoek
van Holland)

6.9 Ep ↑ (lake path, to KP 56)

10.7 At T-jct of KP 56 →, cross
rd and ← via 🚲 (follow
signs to Hoek van Holland
& KP 57, LF 1b)

10.9 1st 🚲 →, after 500 m
follow bend to ←

12.7 1st 🚲 →, cross rd and ↑

13.9 At jct cross rd ↑ onto 🚲
on left-hand side

14.9 Before railway ← via 🚲

17.2 1st 🚲 →

19.5 ← to ferry landing

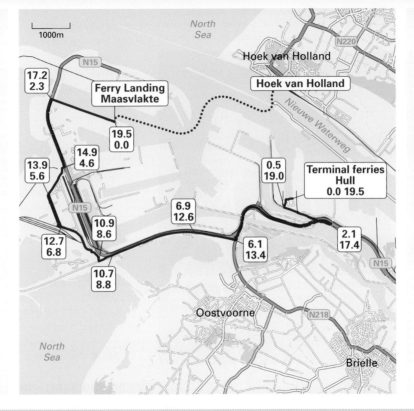

North
Sea

1000m

N15

17.2
2.3

N220

Hoek van Holland

**Ferry Landing
Maasvlakte**

Hoek van Holland

Nieuwe Waterweg

19.5
0.0

14.9
4.6

13.9
5.6

0.5
19.0

**Terminal ferries
Hull
0.0 19.5**

N15

6.9
12.6

10.9
8.6

12.7
6.8

2.1
17.4

10.7
8.8

6.1
13.4

N15

Oostvoorne

N218

North
Sea

Brielle

From Hook to Hull Terminal:

0.0 In Hook, follow signs
"RET Fast Ferry", get off
at Maasvlakte landing, →
via 🚲 on right-hand side
(follow signs to Rotterdam
& KP 56, LF 1a)

2.3 At T-jct ← via 🚲

4.6 Ep → via 🚲 on right

5.6 ↑ via 🚲 on right-hand side
(Dardanellenstraat)

6.8 At jct ← via 🚲 on right

8.6 At T-jct ← via 🚲 on left

8.8 Cross rd → onto 🚲, at
KP 56 1st rd ← (to KP 54)

12.6 Ep ↑ onto 🚲 on right-hand
side (to Rotterdam)

13.4 After rd crossing 1st 🚲 ←
(to Europoort), keep going
↑ next to motorway

17.4 Ep cross rd and → via
🚲 on left-hand side of rd
(to Hull)

19.0 1st 🚲 →, cross rd and
railway (to Hull)

19.5 Hull Ferry Terminal

Section 3 (main): Hook of Holland – Duindorp (18 km)

Hoek van Holland (literally "Corner of Holland") is a small town, marking the southern end of Holland's 118 km (73-mile) sandy beach. It is mainly known for its ferry port. Services to Harwich have been running from here since 1893. The Hoek van Holland beach is a popular destination for Rotterdam folks in summer, as it is only 20 minutes by train from Rotterdam Central Station.

The town is right next to the "Nieuwe Waterweg" shipping canal to Rotterdam. Across this wide canal you will be able to see the docks of Rotterdam Europoort Harbour. Another major feature is the Rotterdam storm surge barrier, "Maeslantkering", 2 miles inland from Hook. It is one of the largest moving structures of the world and consists of two huge doors, which can close off the wide shipping canal entirely.

The route takes you by Hook's town centre before joining one of Holland's most attractive routes: the traffic-free cycling highway through the sand dune reserves of the Dutch coast. Duindorp on the outskirts of The Hague ("Den Haag" in Dutch) is only one hour of pedalling away and there are plenty of opportunities to have a break, like Ter Heyde beach or Kijkduin beach.

One of the two massive doors of the Rotterdam storm surge barrier can easily be reached by bike. Guided tours of the barrier control centre are available. The barrier is 2 miles inland from Hook along the Nieuwe Waterweg canal (see also pages 104 and 107).

0.0 **Cycle on right-hand side!**
Leave ferry terminal ↑
by using main exit, reset
computer at level crossing

0.1 1st rd → via 🚲 on right-hand
side (Prins Hendrikstraat)

0.2 🏠 🍴 🛒 🍴 ⚕
Hoek van Holland

0.4 Just after bike shop, 1st
rd ← via one-way street
with contra flow for cyclists
(Concordia Straat)

0.5 At T-jct ← (1e
Scheepvaartstraat)

0.6 At T-jct → (Rietdijkstraat) and
at T-jct ← (Planciusstraat)

0.8 At T-jct cross rd, → via 🚲 on
left-hand side (Harwichweg)

1.5 At T-jct cross rd, → via
residential street on left-hand
side (Dirk van den Burgweg)

1.7 2nd rd ← via residential
street on left-hand side
(Schelpweg)

2.0 At KP 21 → cross rd, →
via 🚲 on left-hand side
and ← via traffic-free 🚲
(Noordlandsepad, to Kijkduin
& KP 9)

3.0 At jct cross rd, ← via 🚲
on right-hand side, joins rd
further on

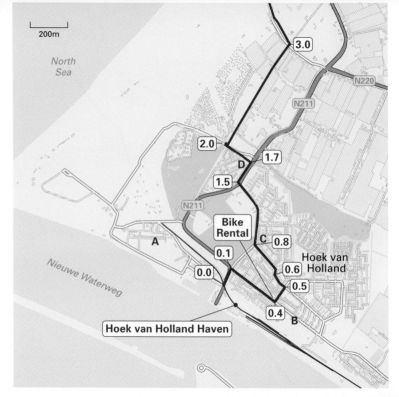

Section 3 (main): Hook of Holland – Duindorp (18 km)

3.6 At end of rd 🚲 ↑ via traffic-free 🚲 (to Kijkduin/ Den Haag)

5.1 At jct with rd ("Strandslag Beukel") ↑ via traffic-free 🚲 (to Monster/Den Haag & KP 9)

7.8 At KP 9 ↑ via traffic-free 🚲 along historic cannons, then ← via rd (Karel Doormanweg, to Strand)

8.0 ⚅🛏 🎋 🏊

Ter Heyde Beach (via steps)

8.0 At steps beach access → (Evertsenstraat)

8.2 2nd rd →, one-way street with contra flow for cyclists (Kortenaerstraat)

8.3 1st rd ← (Van Speykstraat)

8.4 At end of residential area ← via traffic-free 🚲 (to Kijkduin/Scheveningen/Den Haag & KP 6)

10.0 At KP 6 ← via traffic-free 🚲 (to Kijkduin & KP 3)

10.4 Before 🎋 **Schelppad** → via "Fietspad" (to Kijkduin/ Scheveningen/Den Haag & KP 3)

Beach access at Ter Heyde.

600m

North Sea

Schelppad 10.4

10.0

8.2 | 8.4
H

Ter Heyde 8.0

7.8 | 8.3
G

Monster

N211

Strandslag Beukel 5.1

3.6 | F

N211

E | 3.0

's-Gravenzande

Naaldwijk

13.1 At KP 3 ↑ via "Fietspad" (to Kijkduin)

14.0 At jct with main rd ← via 🚲 on right-hand side (to Kijkduin/Scheveningen, LF 1b Noordzeeroute)

14.5 🏄 🛏 📷 🍴 ⛱ 🏖 **The Hague – Kijkduin Beach**

14.5 At the Atlantic Hotel ↑ via "Fietspad" (to Scheveningen, LF 1b Noordzeeroute)

14.8 1st p ← and immediately →, follow main "Fietspad" (to Scheveningen, LF 1b)

17.7 **The Hague – Duindorp** (end of section 3)

Kijkduin is a small area of hotels and eateries, overlooking an unspoilt beach; ideal for a short break!

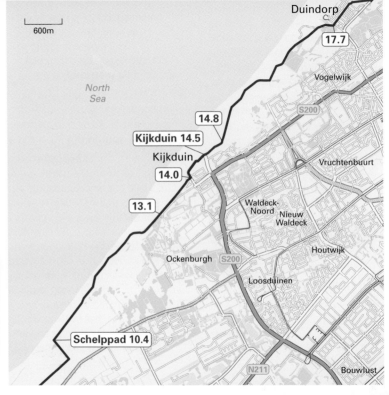

Section 4 (main): The Hague: Duindorp – Water Tower (11 km)

The approach to the Kurhaus Hotel on Scheveningen promenade; the beach awaits you behind this grand building; no cycling on the promenade!

The Hague has plenty to offer. Besides attractions in the city centre there is also the International Court, miniature park Madurodam and the Scheveningen promenade. The route is set up in such a way that it guides you along all major attractions, making it easy to either stay overnight or just to travel through. The following attractions are all within a 10-minute walk from the city centre guarded bike park (open seven days a week; use is recommended!):

- Walk the **Binnenhof**, a medieval square and home to the Dutch government; access opposite the bike park

- Visit the **Mauritshuis**, a world-class museum with paintings of Dutch masters like Rembrandt and Vermeer; admission € 12 pp (Mondays closed); next to Binnenhof

- Have a drink on a cosy terrace on **Plein** (literally "Square"); next to Binnenhof and Mauritshuis Museum

- Wave at the **Dutch prime minister** from the lakeside next to Binnenhof; the dominant rounded feature, sticking slightly into the water, is his designated office room

- Get a glimpse of **Royal Palace Noordeinde**, the office of Queen Beatrix; walk via Gravenstraat and Hoogstraat

- Visit the **Panorama Mesdag Museum**, home to an impressive 360° panorama painting of the Dutch coast at The Hague (former fishing village "Scheveningen"); admission € 6 pp; entrance on Noordeinde Street

0.0 (= 17.7) At the end of 🚲 ↑ (Pluvierstraat, LF 1b Noordzeeroute), later ↗ (Tesselse Straat)

0.8 At T-jct ← via 🚲 on right-hand side (Nieboerweg)

1.0 At T-jct ↖ via 🚲 on right-hand side

1.1 After dam across canal 1st rd → (Kranenburgweg)

1.3 3rd rd ↖ (Willem de Zwijgerlaan)

1.6 At jct with tram tracks ↗ and immediately ↖ (Willem de Zwijgerlaan)

1.8 At next jct ↑ (Willem de Zwijgerlaan)

2.1 At next "give way" jct ↗ (Stadhouderslaan) 🚗

2.4 At jct with lhts ↑ (to Delft/Rotterdam) 🚗🚗

2.7 2nd rd ← across tram tracks (R.J. Schimmelpennicklaan), ↖ via one-way street with contra flow for cyclists, later ↑ (Bickerweg)

3.2 1st rd ← along embassy of Surinam, at T-jct → via 🚲 on right-hand side (Johan de Wittlaan)

3.4 Follow sharp bend ← via 🚲 (to Vredespaleis)

3.9 At next "give way" jct → via 🚲 on right-hand side (Scheveningseweg, to Vredespaleis)

4.1 At jct with lhts ↑ via 🚲 on right-hand side (Carnegielaan)

4.3 🚲 **Vredespaleis (International Court)** Paid for by Scottish millionaire Andrew Carnegie, this "peace palace" was completed in 1913. It houses the International Court of Justice; guided tours by advanced booking (+ 31 70 302 4242).

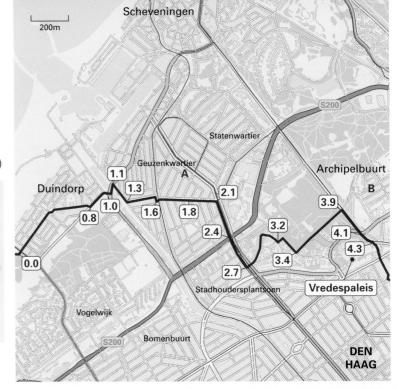

Section 4 (main): The Hague: Duindorp – Water Tower (11 km)

4.3 After International Court entrance ↗ via 🚲 onto different rd

4.4 At jct with lhts ↑ (Anna Paulownastraat)

4.8 At major jct with lhts ← (take control of the left lane, proceed ↑ across jct and turn ← to 🚲 on right-hand side) (Hogewal to Centrum/Wassenaar)

5.1 1st rd → (Noordeinde, to Paleis Noordeinde)

5.2 1st rd ← (Oranjestraat)

5.3 At T-jct → (Park Straat) 🚙, follow rd with bends, use 🚲 where available

5.9 After pond/lake on left-hand side **dismount** and walk ↗ onto square

5.9 🏄 🏨 🏛 🚙 🚲 🍽 🍷 **Den Haag City Centre** Guarded bike park on square; € 0.60 per bike; still lock up your bike and don't leave valuables behind!

5.9 To continue route, face statue of a man on a horse across rd, cross rd and ← resume cycling via 🚲 on right-hand side

6.0 After pond/lake on right-hand side 1st rd → via 🚲 on right-hand side (Lange Vijverberg), ↑

6.6 At major jct ↑ via 🚲 across tram tracks and main rd, ← via 🚲 on right-hand side (to Scheveningen)

7.0 At major jct ↑ across main rd and ↖ via 🚲 on right-hand side, ↑ (to Scheveningen)

8.6 After cycling under viaduct and crossing its slip rd 1st rd ➜ (St Hubertusweg) and immediately ↖ (Kwekerijweg)

8.6 ⮜ **Madurodam:** Legoland-style miniature park with all Dutch well-known buildings on display (trains and planes are included); admission € 15 pp. To get there don't turn into St Hubertusweg, but continue ↑ via 🚲 (entrance after 200 m)

8.8 After office building on left-hand side 1st 🚲 ←

9.1 At end of 🚲 ↑ via residential street (Badhuisweg), keep the main rd on your left-hand side

9.2 At T-jct ↗ (Pompstationweg)

10.1 Cross main rd via lhts, ↑ via "Fietspad" (to Meijendel/ Wassenaar, LF 1b Noordzeeroute)

10.1 ⮜ 🛥 🍴 ⚓ **Scheveningen Kurhaus and Beach:** This is where The Hague takes on famous seaside resorts like Brighton and Blackpool, but in Dutch style. It has a sandy beach (also during high tides) and a complete traffic-free promenade (note: no cycling!). The stylish 19th-century Kurhaus hotel provides grandeur and elegance to the place. To get there don't take the "Fietspad" into the sand dunes, but go ← via 🚲 on right-hand side for 1 km. The main road ends at the back of the Kurhaus hotel, dismount to get to the seafront.

11.0 Water Tower
(end of section 4)

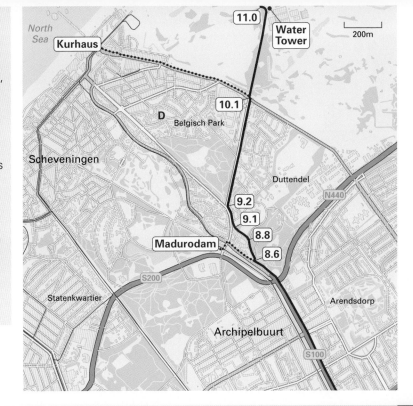

Section 5 (main): Water Tower – Overveen (45 km)

Between The Hague and Haarlem you will encounter the finest section of the Dutch coastal cycle way. The strip of sand dunes is up to 4 miles wide here and the superb cycle path takes you right through its unspoilt heart. Every other mile you'll find a quiet footpath to the beach.

There are also plenty of seaside towns to break up the ride. At Wassenaarse Slag you'll find some eateries and cafés on the beach. Inland you can visit the Duinrell theme park and the Tiki Pool (see page 52).

Katwijk is a relaxed seaside town, although the boulevard and beach can get hugely crowded over the weekends on hot summer days. Most of Katwijk's buildings are reasonably new, as the town suffered badly during WWII. The Germans needed the Katwijk grounds for their "Atlantic Wall", the strategic line of fortifications built to defend against Allied attacks. Most houses within one mile of the beach were cleared. The white lighthouse is one of the few surviving buildings on the boulevard.

The next seaside town is Noordwijk. The town has two long seaside boulevards, not only offering a fantastic sandy beach but also a vibrant nightlife.

The multitude of traffic-free beach access makes the cycling highway along the Dutch coast the very best section of the international North Sea Cycle Route.

Miles of splendid high-quality traffic-free cycling in the Dutch sand dune reserves; a must for anyone who loves cycling!

Beyond Noordwijk you enter the forests of Noordwijkerhout. The pine trees in the sand dunes are not native to the area (the trees were planted to stop sand dune erosion) but offer a great diverse landscape. You'll also find here Dutch micro-infrastructure at its best; paths are either dedicated for cycling, walking, horse riding and even mountain biking! The Noordwijk YHA is pleasantly located on the edge of the forest, perfect for further exploration. Note: Noordwijk town is a 30- to 40-minute bike ride away from this hostel! From the hostel, you can choose to join the alternative route via the tulip fields, a recommendation in April/May, see page 60.

On the main route, beach access Langevelderslag consists of a car park and some eateries. It is important to have a break here as the upcoming stretch between Langevelderslag and Zandvoort is the most remote stretch of the route; there are no facilities until Zandvoort!

Zandvoort, also known as Amsterdam at Sea, is full of hotels, nightlife and trendy beach cafés. Note: the southern boulevard is closed for cyclists heading north, but the northern boulevard to Bloemendaal offers great cycling on a traffic-free path with continuous views over the sea. At Bloemendaal aan Zee the route heads inland to end in the Haarlem suburb Overveen.

Section 5 (main): Water Tower – Overveen (45 km)

0.0 (=11.0) At Water Tower
↑ via traffic-free 🚲 (to
Wassenaar/Katwijk, LF 1b

Noordzeeroute)

6.8 🚰 Free fresh drinking water
pump at T-jct

6.8 ↞ **Duinrell/Tikipool:** Duinrell is a theme park with various rollercoaster and fun rides. The most appealing attraction is the Tiki Pool with 11 world-class slides. It is possible to buy separate tickets for both the theme park and pool. Ticket prices for the pool are based on the time you want to spend in the water, see also www.duinrell.nl. Duinrell is 3 km away from the main route and has ample bike racks at the main entrance. To get there → at the "water pump T-jct" and follow 🚲 to roundabout, there ↗ via 🚲 (Katwijkseweg, to Wassenaar), at jct with lhts → (Storm van 's-Gravesandeweg, to Duinrell), follow Duinrell signs to entrance. To rejoin the main route you'll need to cycle back to the "water pump T-jct".

6.8 At T-jct ← via traffic-free
🚲 (to Strand/Katwijk a Zee/
Noordwijk a Zee, LF 1b)

6.9 ↞ 🚰 🍴 ⛵ **Wassenaarse
Slag** (after 500 m) To get to

the beach, follow 🚲 to end

6.9 1st 🚲 → (to Katwijk a
Zee/Noordwijk a Zee,
LF 1b), cross rd 🚗 and ↖ via
"Fietspad"

8.2 ← 🍴 **Pavilion "The Duinen" (The Dunes):** This hidden gem has great views over the sand dunes and can only be reached by foot/bike.

11.7 At end of 🚲 ← (to Zuid-Boulevard/Noordwijk, LF 1b Noordzeeroute), follow rd onto boulevard. Caution:

There are various "equal junctions" on the boulevard rd; give way to traffic from the right!

13.1 ← 🏠 🅿️ 🍴 🏺 🏌️ **Katwijk aan Zee**

13.7 1st rd ← via rd on dam (Buitensluis, to Noordwijk, LF 1b Noordzeeroute)

This dam on the north end of Katwijk used to mark the most northern point of the Roman Empire in continental Europe; the main flow of the River Rhine reached the North Sea at this point up to about 1,500 years ago.

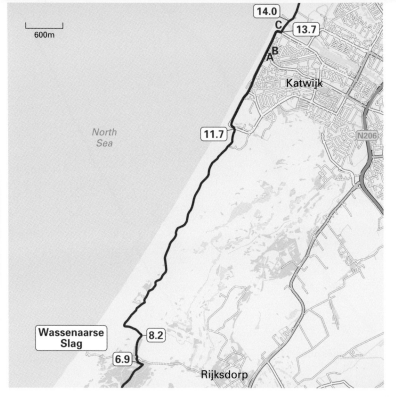

Section 5 (main): Water Tower – Overveen (45 km)

14.0 Just beyond dam ↖ onto traffic-free 🚲 into "Hollands Duin" (Rijwielpad Noordduinen)

16.8 At end of 🚲 ↑ (Kon. Astrid Boulevard). Caution: There are various "equal junctions" on the boulevard rd; give way to traffic from the right!

18.0 At T-jct ← (to Kon. Wilhelmina Boulevard) 🚗🚗

18.3 Just before wide zebra crossing 1st rd ←, one-way street with cyclists contra flow (Paceplein)

18.3 🚶🏠🛏️🍴🚐🎣🚴

Noordwijk aan Zee

Noordwijk was a quiet fishing village for nearly 800 years; now it is a busy holiday resort, visited by more than 1 million visitors per year. The main attraction of the town is of course the beach, although its vicinity to the Dutch tulip fields also attracts flower-minded visitors. An annual highlight (mid-April) is the "Bollenstreek Bloemencorso", a colourful parade of tulip-decorated tractors and themed trailers full of blooming flowers.

19.0 At end of boulevard rd 1st rd ← (Bosweg, to Zandvoort/De Zilk, LF 1b)

19.5 At end of rd ↑ via "Fietspad", traffic-free 🚲 (to De Zilk/Zandvoort, LF 1b)

20.7 At T-jct ← via traffic-free 🚲 (to De Zilk/Zandvoort, LF 1b), keep going ↑

24.4 Stop at 🚲 junction with "mushroom sign" number "21597/001" (on which Zandvoort is 11 km away). Choose between main coastal route or inland alternative route via tulip fields and 🏨 Noordwijk.

Main route via Zandvoort:

24.4 ↖ via gravel "fietspad" (to Zandvoort)

24.7 At T-jct with 🚉 ← via gravel path (to Strand/Langevelderslag/Zandvoort, LF 1b)

25.6 1st 🚲 → (to Langevelderslag/Zandvoort, LF 1b), gravel surface at first, further on bricks pavement

27.1 🛒 🍴 🚉 ⛵ **Langevelderslag Beach**

27.1 ↑ across dead-end rd via traffic-free 🚲 (to Zandvoort, LF 1b), keep going ↑, see next page

Alternative route via tulip fields:

24.4 ↗ via tarmac 🚲 (to Noordwijkerhout), at T-jct ←

24.8 At KP 86 (opposite 🏨 Noordwijk) ↑ via 🚲 on left-hand side (to De Zilk)

25.2 Where 🚲 bends to left (scooter sign) ↑ via rd 🚗

25.9 1st rd → (Wilgendam)

26.9 At T-jct ← (Duinschooten, to Lisse)

27.5 1st 🚲 → (to Lisse & KP 47), at jct ↑ (to KP 48)

28.3 Before tunnel →, ep ←, 1st 🚲 ←, through tunnel and ↑ via rd (Tespellaan, to Lisse & KP 48)

29.2 After golf course 1st rd ← (to KP 48), 1st 🚲 →

30.2 Jct at KP 48; for Keukenhof → via 🚲 (2 km; see page 62), otherwise ↑ (see page 63)

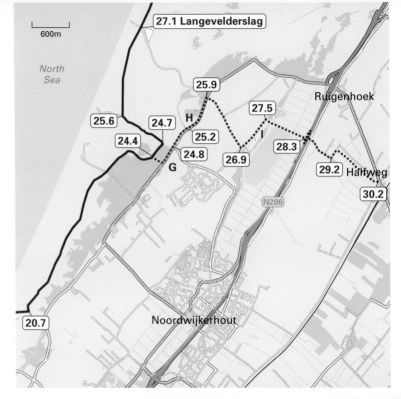

600m

North Sea

27.1 Langevelderslag

Ruigenhoek

25.9

27.5

25.6

24.7

H

25.2

I

28.3

24.4

24.8

26.9

29.2 Halfweg

G

30.2

N206

20.7

Noordwijkerhout

Section 5 (main): Water Tower – Overveen (45 km)

30.4 ⟨ Provincial border

This stretch is the most remote section of the coastal route. The only significant landmark is the border between North and South Holland. Some explanations: when the Republic of The Netherlands was founded back in 1588, the country consisted of seven provinces. One of these provinces was Holland, other well-known provinces being Zeeland (New Zealand is named after this province) and Friesland (home of the Frisian cow). During the 17th century the province of Holland became the most powerful, creating a trademark of its own. "Made in Holland" is still a popular trademark, being used all over The Netherlands, but it is not the official name of the country! The other provinces took

a stand in 1840 and Holland was forced to divide into two provinces to balance its power with the other Dutch provinces, explaining this border between South and North Holland.

Another thing: The Hague was originally the capital of the country, but in 1795 Napoleon demanded that Amsterdam should be the capital. When the French occupation ended this status remained unchanged, but the seat of the government returned to The Hague ...

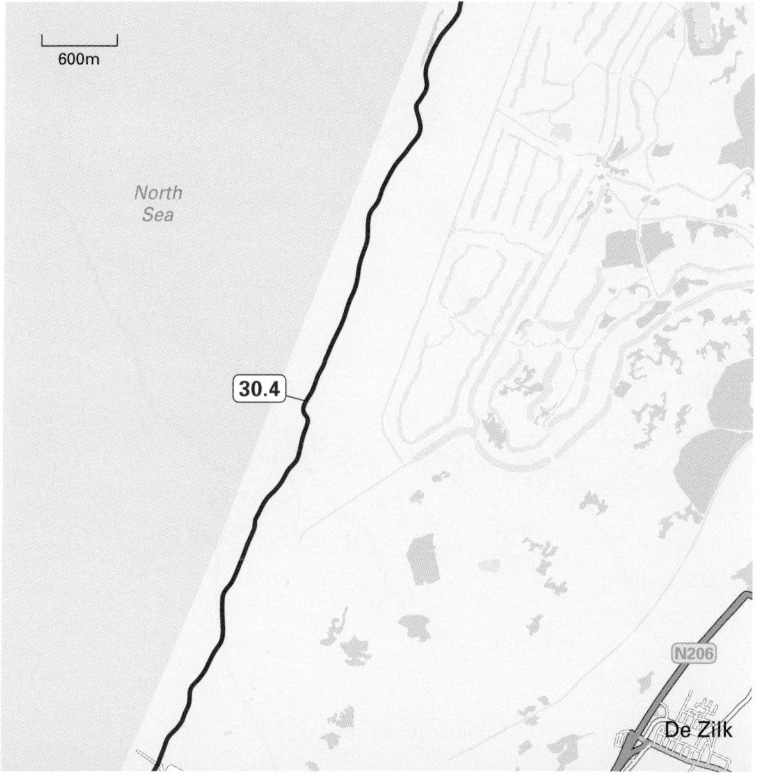

600m

North
Sea

30.4

N206

De Zilk

34.6 At end of 🚲 → (Brederodestraat, to Haarlem)

35.4 At roundabout ↑ (Marisstraat, to Station)

35.7 At T-jct (next to high tower) ↗ (Thorbeckestraat)

35.8 At roundabout ↑ (to Station/Circuit) 🚗🚗

35.9 ⚑🚲🍴🏕⛵ **Zandvoort** Guarded Bike Park on left (next to Holland Casino)

36.5 Where main rd rejoins coast as boulevard rd use 🚲 on right-hand side

36.9 Dismount near "Strandhotel Zandvoort" (big building on right) to cross rd ↑ onto 🚲 along beach on left-hand side of main carriageway

39.6 ⚑🚲🍴⛵ **Bloemendaal aan Zee**

39.6 Just beyond jct "Parnassiaweg" cross main rd ↑ onto 🚲 on right-hand side of main carriageway

43.2 Beyond sign "maximum speed 50 km/h" and just before sign "Duincentrum De Zandwaaier" → via dead-end rd (Tetterodeweg), at gate ↖ via 🚲

43.5 ⚑🚲 **Duincentrum De Zandwaaier** Sand Dune Nature Reserve Educational Centre with various exhibitions on vegetation and wildlife; pedestrian access from bike racks next to path.

43.6 At end of 🚲 ↑ onto rd

43.9 At jct cross main rd ↑ (Tetterodeweg)

44.3 On arrival in "Overveen" ↗ onto 🚲, rejoin rd beyond jct (Tetterodeweg)

44.7 🚲🚲 **Overveen** (end of section 5)

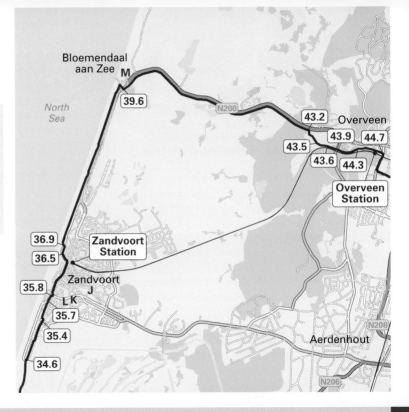

Section 6 (main): Overveen – Haarlem (3 km)

Haarlem is a compact historic Dutch city with a medieval canal layout. In English, the place is known as "Harlem" (like the district in New York City).

By the 10th century Haarlem was an established place, and by the 14th century it had become a major Dutch city, more important than Amsterdam or Rotterdam. Haarlem had a great boom period during the Dutch Golden Age, with impressive historical buildings as a result. The Belgium-born painter Frans Hals grew up in Haarlem and Haarlem-born Laurens Janszoon Coster is believed to be the inventor of the printing press, well before German Johann Gutenberg presented his prototype to the world. An intriguing visitor was Mozart, who is believed to have played the organ in St. Bavo Church on Haarlem's central square, "Grote Markt". During the 18th and 19th centuries Haarlem remained an important city, with its beer and textile industries booming. It also became increasingly important as a trading centre for tulips. The actual flower trading has now moved to huge flower auctions near Amsterdam and The Hague, but the annual flower parade from Noordwijk still ends in Haarlem (see also pages 54 and 60).

The best way to take in Haarlem is to have a stroll through its old streets. Don't miss the scenic "hofjes", small inner courts in between private houses, originally designated for the retired. Most of these are private property, but some are open to the public. Get the leaflet "Haarlemse Hofjeswandeling" from the Dutch Tourist Board VVV for a walking map showing the "hofjes".

Museums in Haarlem are also worth a visit. The Frans Hals Museum displays an impressive collection of paintings by the master, as well as other lesser-known Dutch masters from Haarlem. The Teylers Museum opened in 1784 and is the oldest museum in The Netherlands. The historic building is worth a look in itself. Most of the collection has been unchanged since the 18th and 19th centuries, and varies from minerals to scientific instruments. Both museums charge about € 8 pp and are closed on Mondays.

Note: most Haarlem accommodation doesn't have space to store bicycles overnight. Safe overnight bike parking is available in Smedestraat, open from 7 am until midnight, right next to Grote Markt. Charges are approx € 0.70 per day and an additional € 0.50 for an overnight stay. The YHA provides overnight bike parking, but is located well beyond the city centre (see section 8, page 67).

The *"Grote Markt"* with
St. Bavo Church.

For a more detailed map of
Haarlem's city centre, see
page 65 (the main route is
highlighted by a dotted line).

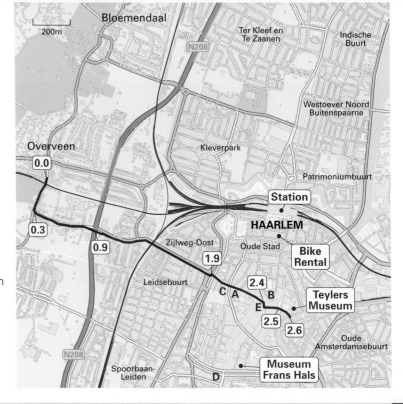

0.0 (= 44.7) At T-jct → (Bloemendaalseweg, to Haarlem/Den Haag), cross railway level crossing and join 🚲 on right-hand side

0.3 At rndabt ← (Zijlweg, to Haarlem/Den Haag) 🚗, use 🚲 where available

0.9 At major jct with lhts ↑ via 🚲 (to Centrum)

1.9 At jct with lhts ↑ via foot/ cycle bridge across canal, at other side cross ↑ into one-way street with cyclists contra flow (Zijlstraat), keep going ↑

2.4 🚶 🏠 🏨 🍽 ☕ 🍴 🔧
Haarlem (Grote Markt)

2.4 Facing the cathedral and main statue on the square "Grote Markt", → in front of the cathedral (Lepelstraat) and immediately ← (Spekstraat)

2.5 At next jct ↑ (Damstraat)

2.6 **Spaarne River at "De Waag"** (end of section 6)

Section 7 (tulips alternative): Voorhout – Haarlem (27 km)

This alternative route takes you across the Dutch tulip fields, which are generally blooming from early April until late May. You can join this route at Voorhout station (if you choose not to cycle the main route between The Hague and Haarlem) or from the main route north of Noordwijk (section 5). In this situation you first follow instructions on page 55 to join in at page 63.

Although often displayed in pictures and paintings, the Dutch tulip fields or bulb fields only cover a small geographical area between the Dutch cities of Leiden and Haarlem, known as the "bollenstreek" (bulb region). The tulip is not native to The Netherlands and was brought to Western Europe by Carolus Clusius, who saw his first bulbs flowering on Dutch soil in 1594. The flower quickly became known for its beautiful colours. During the Dutch Golden Age the tulip was a fashionable symbol of wealth, with prices for a single tulip bulb rocketing up to 10 times the annual salary of a skilled craftsman. People have been intrigued by the flower ever since and Dutch marketing has ensured The Netherlands are forever associated with the tulip, although there are many other areas in the world where the tulip is cultivated.

The ride between Voorhout and Haarlem provides you with plenty of views of commercial bulb fields, where tulips are cultivated for the world market. To enjoy the colours in a parkland setting you have to visit the Keukenhof Gardens near the town of Lisse. This is the biggest flower

garden of the world with roughly 7 million bulbs being planted every year, to be gazed at by approximately 800,000 people over an eight-week period every spring. The Keukenhof Gardens are about halfway along the route between Voorhout and Haarlem. You should allow two to four hours for a visit; admission is about € 15 pp. See also www.keukenhof.nl.

Another tulip-related attraction worth visiting is the Panorama Tulipland on the outskirts of Voorhout. This is the creation of Dutch painter Leo van den Ende who is working on a circular panorama painting of the Dutch bulb fields. The painting is intended to show how the Dutch tulip area looked on a spring day in the 1950s. You can enjoy a drink whilst observing Mr van den Ende at work (admission € 6 pp).

Beyond the bulb fields, on the outskirts of Haarlem, you'll pass the Cruquius Steam Engine Pumping Station. This machine was, along with two other steam engines, responsible for emptying the vast "Haarlemmermeer" (Haarlem Lake) of its water and reclaiming the land. It took over three years of pumping until the area was declared "dry land" in 1852. This area is now home to the new towns Nieuw Vennep/Hoofddorp and Amsterdam Schiphol Airport. Modern pumping stations have taken on the continuous task of keeping the water levels in this area down whilst the Cruquius Steam Engine has been restored to its former glory. Visit the Cruquius Museum to learn how steam power took on the challenge of preventing Amsterdam from flooding, and experience on the factory floor how steam-driven arms scoop the water 5 metres up from one canal to the other (open daily, admission € 8 pp). For information about Haarlem, see page 58.

The Cruquius Steam Engine is an "Anchor Point" on the European Route of Industrial Heritage (www.erih.net).

Section 7 (tulips alternative): Voorhout – Haarlem (27 km)

0.0 Leave Voorhout Station at the level crossing on the southern end of the platforms, ← via 🚲 on left-hand side, after 30 m cross rd via zebra and continue via 🚲 on right-hand side

0.1 At rndabt ↑ (Jacoba van Beierenweg, to Noordwijkerhout & KP 59), keep going ↑

0.9 ⬱ 📷 **Panorama Tulipland**

1.1 At T-jct → via 🚲 on right-hand side (Zuidelijke Randweg, to Leiden)

1.5 At rndabt ← via 🚲 crossings (Engelse Laan)

1.7 At T-jct ← (Prinsenweg, to KP 59)

2.9 Cross main rd 🚗🚗 ↑ (Torenlaan)

4.0 After bend to left 1st rd → (Akervoorderlaan)

4.5 1st rd ← (Achterweg-Zuid, to KP 55)

5.2 At KP 55 1st rd ← (to KP 49)

6.2 At T-jct → (Loosterweg-Zuid, to KP 49) 🚗

7.7 Just before start 30 km/h zone follow rd layout with sharp bend to ← (to KP 49) 🚗

8.9 ⬱ 📷 🍴 **Keukenhof Gardens** At T-jct (KP 49) → (entrance after 100 m on left)

8.9 To continue route ← at T-jct (KP 49) via 🚲 on left-hand side (Stationsweg, to KP 40)

10.4 📷 🍴 **De Verloren Koffer** (restaurant)

10.5 Jct KP 48 after level crossing (reset computer)

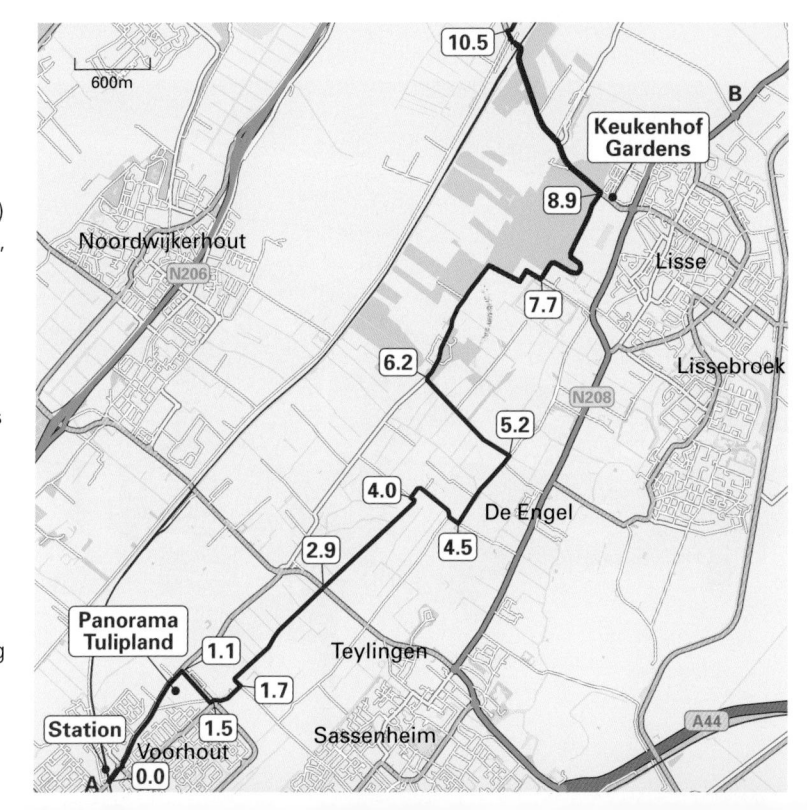

0.0 (= 10.5 or 30.2) At KP 48 cross main rd 🚗 northbound (Leidse Vaart, to De Zilk & Kp 11)

1.0 🌲 **Leidse Vaart** *(overlooking tulip fields)*

2.5 At T-jct (KP 11) → via 🚲 on right-hand side and after bridge ← (Noorder Leidse Vaart, to KP 16)

4.5 At T-jct (KP 16) → (Margrietenlaan, to KP 17) 🚗

4.8 At KP 17 1st rd ↖ (Nieuwe Weg, to KP 18)

6.0 At T-jct → via 🚲 on right-hand side and at KP 18 1st rd ← (Bethlehemlaan, to KP 87)

6.2 1st rd ← (Zandlaan)

6.9 At T-jct ← and 1st rd → (Schoollaan, to KP 87)

7.0 1st rd → (Harp), at next jct ↗

7.2 1st "fietspad" ↗ and ↑ via rd (De Ruyterlaan, to Zwaanshoek & KP 56)

7.9 Just before end of rd → (Jacob van Heemskerklaan, to Zwaanshoek)

8.1 1st rd ← (to KP 56)

8.2 At T-jct → (to Zwaanshoek & KP 56) 🚗🚗

8.3 At lhts after bridge (KP 56) ← (to Cruquius & KP 52) 🚗

Keukenhof Gardens

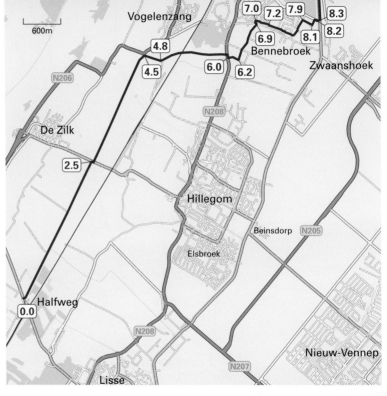

Section 7 (tulips alternative): Voorhout – Haarlem (27 km)

11.0 At jct 1st rd ↖, one-way rd with contra flow for cyclists

11.4 At jct 🚗🚗 ↑ via 🚲 crossing with lhts (Ringvaart Cruquius Dijk, to Cruquius Museum)

11.6 ⟨ **Cruquius Museum**

11.6 Opposite museum ←, take ferry "Stroomboot" (free, 1 Apr – 30 Sep, if service is cancelled ↑ for 200 m, cross footbridge ← and ← to ferry landing)

11.6 At other side of canal ↑ (Zuid Schalkwijkerweg)

13.0 At jct ↖ (Zuid Schalkwijkerweg, to KP 74)

13.3 At KP 74 ↑ via 🚲 tunnel (to Centrum & KP 85), keep going ↑ via Zuid Schalkwijkerweg

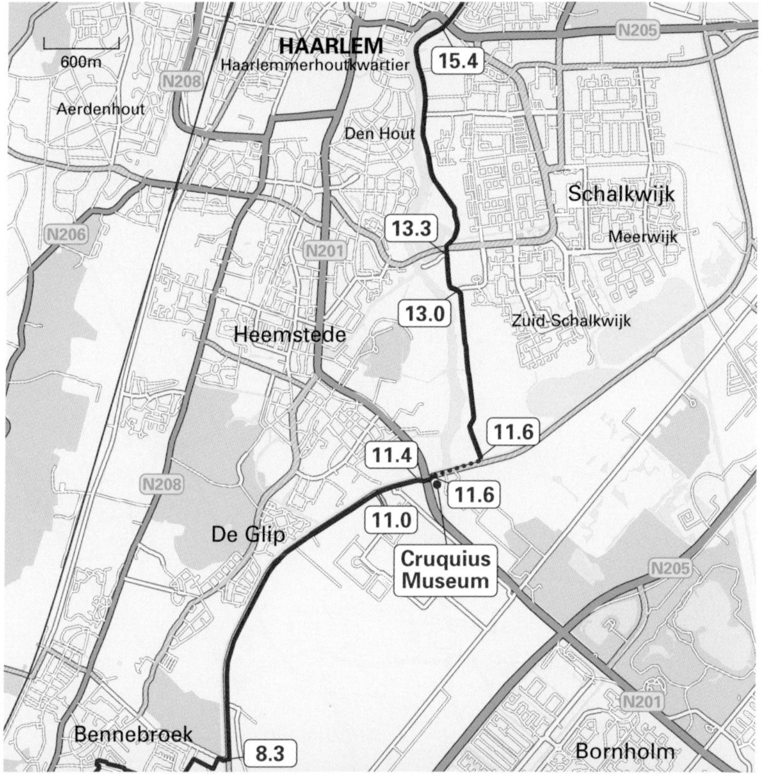

15.4 At jc with lhts (KP 85) 🚗🚗 ↑ via 🚲 on left-hand side of rd (to Centrum, along Spaarne River)

16.2 At lhts ↑ to 🚲 on right-hand side and cross main Spaarne River Bridge

16.3 After bridge at KP 90 ↗ via 🚲 on right-hand side of rd (to KP 22, along Spaarne River), keep going ↑ via river route

16.8 Historic building "De Waag", end of section 7

On this map the main route from Zandvoort is highlighted by a dotted line. Accommodation letters refer to section 6.

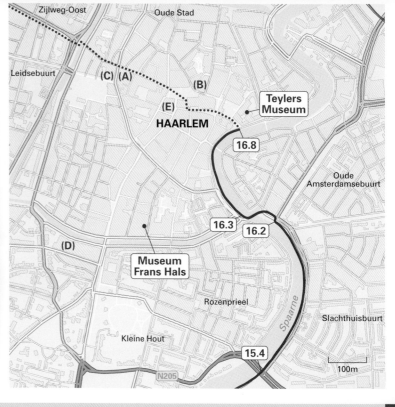

Section 8 (main): Haarlem – Amsterdam (42 km)

Windmill spotting at Zaanse Schans.

This ride takes you via the Spaarne River to the scenic village of Spaarndam. Above a lock in the old Spaarndam sea wall you'll pass a statue of the legendary fictitious boy Hans Brinker, who put his finger in a Dutch dyke to prevent the land from flooding. From here you cycle to a free ferry across the North Sea shipping canal, taking you into an area known as "Waterland". In Waterland you'll find many fine traditional wooden buildings, typical for this part of the country.

"Zaanse Schans", one of Holland's premium windmill reserves, is located in the heart of Waterland, halfway between Haarlem and Amsterdam. You'll not only find windmills here, but also various preserved Dutch traditional buildings, a cheese farm and a clog factory. Most buildings at Zaanse Schans have been relocated from elsewhere to be preserved here. Admission to the Zaanse Schans area is free, but there are individual charges for buildings you'd like to see from the inside.

From Zaanse Schans to Amsterdam you'll cycle mostly traffic-free through the Twiske Nature Reserve, an empty low-lying area with bushy reedlands. Note: you won't run into any pubs or eateries until you arrive in Amsterdam.

0.0 (= 2.6 or 16.8) At jct along Spaarne River next to "De Waag" head north via one-way street with contra flow 🚲 on right-hand side (next to water)

0.6 At jct with lhts ↑ via 🚲 on right-hand side (next to water, to Bloemendaal/Alkmaar)

1.2 At jct with lhts ↑ via 🚲 on right-hand side (next to water, to Spaarndam/Alkmaar) 🚗

3.3 At T-jct with lhts ← via 🚲 on left-hand side (to Spaarndam/Alkmaar)

3.6 At jct with lhts → (Spaarndamseweg, to Spaarndam), becomes one-way rd with contra flow for cyclists, follow river route ↗ (for 🏠 ← at lhts)

5.5 In Spaarndam, dismount on narrow paved street at historic harbour to walk ↑ over narrow footbridge, keep walking ↗ (Oostkolk), at end walk up steep slope to

5.6 ⟨ 🚂 **Spaarndam – Hans Brinker Statue**

5.6 Start/End link IJmuiden Ferry Route, see page 39

5.6 At Hans Brinker Statue → onto dyke rd 🚗

5.9 After bridge ↖ via 🚲 on left-hand side (to Amsterdam/Zaanstad & KP 11)

9.5 At KP 11 ↑ via 🚲 (to Halfweg/Amsterdam)

9.6 Dismount at 🚢 ferry landing, ← onto ferry, board via pedestrian area on right-hand side (🚲 free)

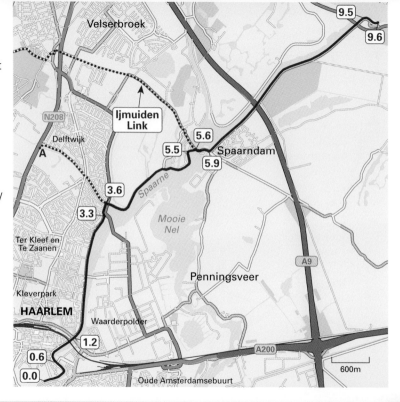

Section 8 (main): Haarlem – Amsterdam (42 km)

9.7 Join 🚲 on right-hand side (to KP 10)

9.8 At KP 10 ↑ via 🚲 on right-hand side (to Nauerna/Westzaan-Zuid & KP 67)

9.9 1st rd → via 🚲 (to Nauerna/Westzaan-Zuid)

10.1 At private gate ↖ via traffic-free 🚲 (to KP 67)

11.4 At end of 🚲 ↗ via dyke road (to Nauerna)

11.9 🍴 Nauerna (pub "The Vlonder")

12.0 After bridge immediately ← via dead-end rd (except 🚲), becomes traffic-free 🚲 along canal

14.5 1st rd → (Watermolenstraat)

14.8 After bridge, 1st rd ← (Oranjeboomstraat)

15.0 At T-jct ← (Torenstraat)

15.2 1st rd → (Kerkstraat), keep going ↑ via Raadhuisstraat and Teunis Slagterstraat

15.3 🍴 Westzaan

15.6 At T-jct ← (Jacobus van Waertstraat), short 🚲

15.7 At T-jct ← (Prinsenhofstraat), immediately ↑ via 🚲, cross main rd, and → via 🚲 on left-hand side

16.2 Where main rd veers off to the right ↑ via 🚲 on left-hand side (to Zaandijk/Zaanse Schans)

17.3 At T-jct ← via 🚲 (to Zaandijk/Koog a/d Zaan)

17.6 At jct with lhts ↑ across 1st 🚲 crossing, then immediately → via 2nd 🚲 crossing onto residential rd (Jan Mulderstraat, to Koog a/d Zaan)

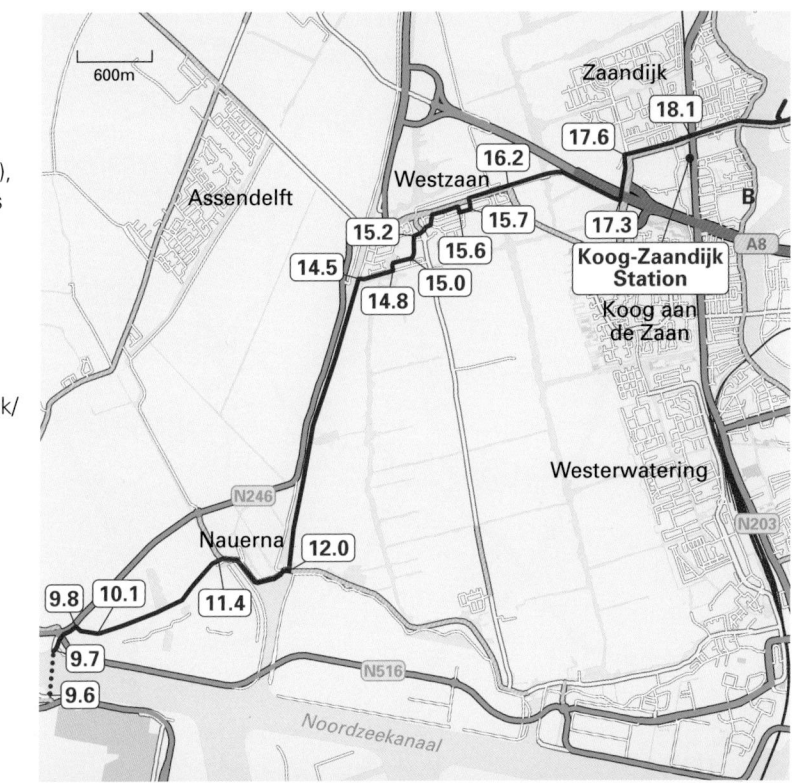

18.1 Immediately after railway level crossing ⚠ via 🚲 crossing with lhts (to Zaanse Schans/Purmerend), follow signs to Zaanse Schans through residential area to 🚲

19.2 🚻 🍴 Zaanse Schans Windmill Reserve Best place to park bicycles is the small square on the river side before the first windmill, next to the river cruises. The Zaan River area has been an industrial area for centuries, fuelled by wind power. The Zaan River area was home to thousands of industrial windmills, but today only 13 mills remain. Six of these can be found at Zaanse Schans; two saw mills, two oil mills, a paint mill and a mustard mill. Climb the steps of at least one running windmill to experience the creaking sounds and majestic force of wind power!

19.2 Turn around in the same direction you came from

19.4 At main rd ← via 🚲 on left-hand side (to Oostzaan, Het Twiske, Purmerend & KP 50)

21.2 At jct with lhts cross main rd → 🚗 (to Purmerend/Het on bridge across Zaan River

19.0 Immediately after bridge ← (to Zaanse Schans) and immediately ← via scenic paved rd

Twiske & KP 50)

21.4 🍴 Haaldersbroek (pub "'t Heerenhuis")

21.4 1st rd ↖, stay on rd with canal on right-hand side, see sign "Fietsers richting Purmerend"

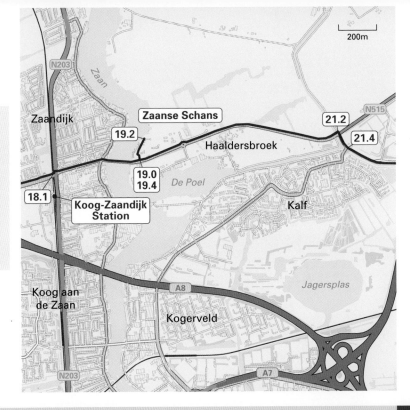

Section 8 (main): Haarlem – Amsterdam (42 km)

22.3 At KP 50 ↑ (to Neck/ Purmerend & KP 33)

24.3 Take 1st rd → (Westerdwarsweg, to KP 33)

25.0 After bridge ← via "Fietspad" (to KP 33)

26.9 At jct ↗ via dyke rd (to Amsterdam/Purmerend)

27.0 1st ⮞ → "Fietspad" (Wormerpad Nrs 5-3-2, to "Doorgaand Verkeer")

27.3 After railway level crossing ↘ via "Fietspad" (to Oostzaan/ Zaanstad/Amsterdam)

28.8 At rd crossing ↑ via "Fietspad", turn immediately ← (to Het Twiske/Den Ilp & KP 15)

29.0 1st ⮞ → (to Het Twiske & KP 15)

30.0 At jct ← (to Den Ilp/ Infocentrum & KP 15),

keep going ↑ via traffic-free ⮞ to "Boerderij" (including two rd crossings)

32.0 At T-jct ← via traffic-free ⮞ (to Landsmeer/Amsterdam/ Boerderij)

32.2 At jct ↑ via ⮞ (to KP 20, LF 7b)

32.6 At jct ↑ via ⮞ (ignore signs for KP 20 & LF 7b)

33.1 At T-jct → and 1st ⮞ ← (to Amsterdam, see mushroom sign 25216), keep going ↑ (to KP 19)

33.9 At KP 19 ← via traffic-free ⮞ (Het Luijendijkje, to Landsmeer/Amsterdam/ Broek in Waterland), keep going ↑, passing under Amsterdam motorway orbital into suburbs and across bus route

35.6 At end of traffic-free ℮ ← via residential rd (to Centrum/ Buikslotermeerplein)

35.8 At T-jct ← via road with cycle lanes 🚗, keep following this rd ↖ (Eudorinastraat) 🚗

36.2 At jct → (Kadoelenweg, to Amsterdam)

36.8 1st rd ← (to Centrum/ Buikslotermeerplein), becomes traffic-free ℮

37.3 After traditional bridge 1st rd → (to Centrum/ Buikslotermeerplein)

37.5 After city farm buildings ↖ via ℮

37.7 At T-jct ↖ via "low level" ℮ on left-hand side of embankment (to Centrum/ Buikslotermeerplein)

38.1 After passing through tunnel 1st ℮ →, immediately leading through another tunnel, ↑ via ℮ along shops and across rd

39.0 After passing through another tunnel at next ℮ jct ← (to Buikslotermeerplein/ Schellingwoude)

39.2 ⛵ **Buiksloterdijk** (traditional dyke houses)

39.7 At end of ℮ ↑ via rd for 15 metres, then → via traffic-free ℮ along canal (to Centrum, LF 7a), keep going ↑ via canal route

41.9 At T-jct ← via ℮ on left-hand side (to Centrum) Busy traffic flow from opposite direction possible!

42.2 Dismount at ferry landing, board ferry Caution: bike theft and pick-pocketing possible!

42.2 ⛵ 🏠 🏛 🍽 📷 🍴 ⚓ **Amsterdam** (end of section 8)

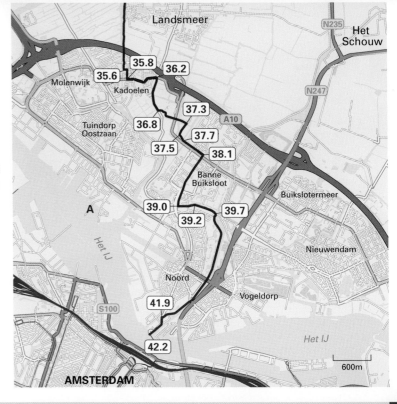

Section 9 (extra): Amsterdam Round Trip (20 or 28 km)

It is impossible to sum up all the things to see and do in Amsterdam in the context of this guide; so we have to limit ourselves to cycling issues. We don't recommend cycling in the historic city centre, as this can be quite stressful. What we do recommend though is a circular ride away from the city centre, along the scenic Amstel River, through Amsterdam's parks and back via the beautiful Jordaan area. This route makes a lovely cycling morning, afternoon or even a full day!

Don't underestimate the risk of bike theft in Amsterdam. Use a guarded bike park where possible, like Mac Bike at Central Station. Mac Bike is located at the front side of the station, at both ends of the building. Charges are approx € 1.10 per day; if you wish to park overnight you need to pay for two days. Note: all our routes start/end at Central Station, so it is easy to leave your bike at Mac Bike, take your luggage and go by foot or tram to your accommodation. In this respect we can recommend the easy-access and fun Amstel Botel Hotel, a floating hotel in the IJ-harbour (no indoor bike storage!). You only have to board the free pedestrian ferry between Central Station and "NDSM-Werf" (a pleasant quay with cafés and eateries) to get there (travel time 15 minutes).

Amsterdam is also served by three YHA hostels, offering the best budget accommodation available in the city. Hostel "Stadsdoelen" is closest to Central Station and our main route. Both hostels

"Stadsdoelen" and "Vondelpark" are on our Amsterdam round trip and have direct access to the city centre. Hostel "Zeeburg" is a couple of kilometres away. Use section 10 towards Maarssen to get there; a bit of map reading is required for the last kilometre (see page 81). There is also a campsite close to the city centre; see the northern route (section 15, page 109).

0.0 (= 42.2) At Amsterdam Central Station, go to main ferry landing and head east via 🚲 along water (to A'dam Oost/Almere & KP 5)

0.5 1st 🚲 crossing → via tunnel with 🚲 on left-hand side (to Central Station, LF 2a Stedenroute)

0.6 Immediately after tunnel cross ↑ onto 🚲 on right-hand side on bridge

0.7 At jct with lhts ↑ via 🚲 on right-hand side of rd (next to canal, to Hilversum, LF 2a Stedenroute)

1.1 Ep → around historic town gate (Nieuwmarkt) and ↑ on right-hand side of canal (Kloveniersburgwal)

1.7 3rd bridge ← and ↑ via 🚲 (Staalstraat, keep following 🚲) Caution: give way to traffic from the right!

The Amstel River gave Amsterdam its name.

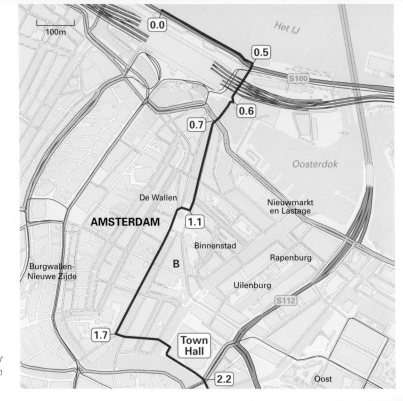

Section 9 (extra): Amsterdam Round Trip (20 or 28 km)

2.2 Ep cross main rd 🚗🚗
↑ onto one-way rd with
cyclists contra flow (Amstel,
to Hilversum, LF 2a)

This is the finest stretch of
cycling in Amsterdam city
centre. You'll pass great historic
monuments like the famous
"Magere Brug" (literally
"skinny bridge". You also pass
the Royal Theatre Carre on your
left. This theatre was built as a
permanent circus at the end of
the 19th century and although
it still hosts a circus around
Christmas, it is mostly the
stage for major Dutch comedy
and music shows. Opposite
the theatre you'll see the old
Amstel locks. At the next
junction you'll pass the Amstel
Hotel, the most expensive hotel
in town.

2.9 At T-jct ← via 🚲 in middle
of rd, immediately → (Prof
Tulpplein, to Hilversum,
LF 2a Stedenroute), follow
river route ↑ (via subway,
later cross tram tracks,
sometimes 🚲 or one-way
with contra flow)

4.5 At jct with lhts → via bridge
and 🚲 on right-hand side
(Berlagebrug, to Amstelveen)

4.6 After bridge at lhts ↑ via 🚲
crossing and ← via another
🚲 crossing onto 🚲 on right-
hand side (Amsteldijk,
to Amstelveen)

5.2 After "Riverstaete" building
at lhts 1st rd ↖ via 🚲
crossing (Amsteldijk, to
Amstelveen)

6.2 At jct ↑ (Amsteldijk, to Amstelveen), keep going ↑ via river route

7.6 ⬉ **Amstelpark** (entrance, no cycling in park!)

8.0 At rndabt ↑ (Amsteldijk, to Amsterdamse Bos) 🚗

8.0 ⬉ **Rieker Molen windmill & Rembrandt Statue**

8.2 ☕ 🍴 **Klein Kalfje**

8.2 1st rd → at KP 65 (Kalfjeslaan, to A'damse Bos & KP 84, later traffic-free 🚲

9.9 2nd 🚲 bridge ← and → via 🚲 tunnel (to Amsterdamse Bos & KP 84)

10.0 After tunnel ↗ via 🚲 bridge and ← (to Amsterdamse Bos & KP 84)

Away from it all in the Amsterdam Wood (Amsterdamse Bos)

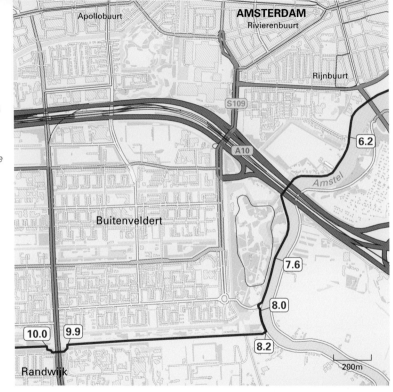

Section 9 (extra): Amsterdam Round Trip (20 or 28 km)

10.8 At jct with lhts ↑ (Nieuwe Kalfjeslaan, to Aalsmeer)

11.0 Stop at 2nd jct after level crossing (tram tracks) Choose here between main route or shortcut:

11.0 **Shortcut:** → (to "Bezoekerscentrum"), at end of rd ↗ via "fietspad", at jct KP 83 → (to KP 81), at ⸖ **Visitor Centre** ← cross rd and → via 🚲 by ⸖ 🍴 **De Bosbaan**, continue after 19.1 km below

11.0 **Main route:** ↑ via rd (to "Amsterdamse Manage")

11.9 2nd "fietspad" → (to "Amsterdamse Manage")

12.2 At jct → via tarmac 🚲 (to "Geitenboerderij")

13.2 2nd tarmac 🚲 → (to "Geitenboerderij")

13.8 1st tarmac 🚲 → (to "Boerderij Meerzicht"),

keep going ↑ via tarmac 🚲

14.5 ⸖ ⸖ **Geitenboerderij** (city farm after 50 m on right)

15.5 At T-jct ← via tarmac 🚲 (to "Boerderij Meerzicht")

15.7 1st tarmac 🚲 ← (to "Boerderij Meerzicht")

16.0 At T-jct ← via tarmac 🚲 (to "Boerderij Meerzicht")

16.1 Cross rd 🚗 ↑ via tarmac 🚲, also at next jct ↑

16.5 At T-jct ← via tarmac 🚲 (to "Bezoekerscentrum")

16.7 ⸖ 🍴 **Boerderij Meerzicht** (pancake restaurant)

16.7 1st tarmac "fietspad" → (to "Bezoekerscentrum")

19.1 ⸖ ⸖ 🍴 **De Bosbaan & Visitor Centre** (300 m; →)

19.1 Via wide 🚲 ↑ (to Amsterdam), (from shortcut →)

19.2 At level crossing 1st 🚲 ← (to Amsterdam-West)

19.4 Ep ↑ via rd (to Amsterdam-West), join 🚲 on right-hand side after 200 m, keep going ↑

20.0 At embankment of motorway cross slip rd ↑ via 🚲 tunnel on left-hand side of tram tracks

20.4 Cross rd ↑ via 🚲 (Piet Kranenburgpad)

20.8 ⟨ 🚶 🍴 **Olympic Stadium** (via footbridge; →) This stadium hosted the 1928 Olympic Games and has recently been restored to its former glory.

21.1 Ep ↑ via rd, keep to 🚲 markings Extreme caution: various tram tracks in rd surface!

21.5 At T-jct ← cycle on rd (Caution; tram tracks!)

21.6 1st rd ← (Vlietstraat)

22.0 🚲 **Zeilstraat** (shops)

22.0 Cross rd 🚗🚗 ↑ (Schinkelkade) Caution: give way to traffic from the right!

22.5 At end of rd ↖ and immediately → via 🚲 (Schinkel Havenkade)

22.6 At lhts cross rd 🚗🚗 ↑ into ⟨ **Vondelpark**, follow 🚲 signs ↑ (to Centrum/A'dam Noord) Caution: busy shared route; try to keep to the right and overtake pedestrians on left where possible.

The Vondelpark was created in 1875. The ANWB (the Dutch AA, very much a cyclist's organisation at the time) part-funded the project and finally reserved the right to cycle in the park in 1897 after many years of restrictions and heated debates.

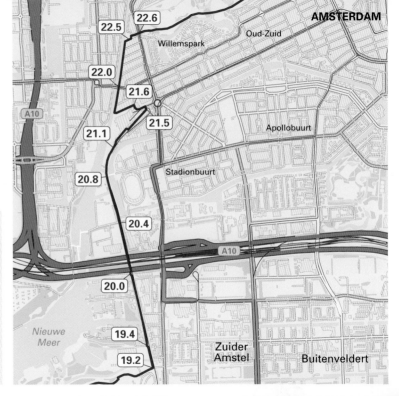

AMSTERDAM

Section 9 (extra): Amsterdam Round Trip (20 or 28 km)

24.1 🅿 🍴 **Vertigo** (park café 50 m; ← before tunnel)

24.6 At end of park cross rd 🚗🚗 ↑ via lhts onto 🚲 bridge (to Centrum/A'dam Noord)

24.7 Ep ← via 🚲 on right-hand side (to Zaanstad) and immediately → (Klein Gartman Plantsoen) with ⇐ 🅿 🍴 **Leidse Plein** on left-hand side, keep going ↑ (Leidsekruisstraat)

24.9 2nd rd ← (Lange Leidsedwarsstraat)

25.0 Dismount at next jct and walk → into shopping street 🚋 🅿 🍴 **Leidse Straat**

25.1 After bridge immediately ← (Prinsengracht), resume cycling and keep going ↑ Caution: dead slow at jcts; give way to traffic from the right!

The Prinsengracht is one of three concentric half-circled canals around Amsterdam's medieval city centre, constructed during the 17th century (the others being Keizersgracht and Herengracht). These canals were dug as part of an ambitious city extension plan, which turned out to be sufficient until the mid-19th century. The three main canals and the canals in the Jordaan area (northwest of the Anne Frank House) are UNESCO World Heritage Sites.

26.1 At lhts cross rd 🚗🚗 ↑ (Prinsengracht)

26.2 ⛪ **Anne Frank's House,** keep going ↑

27.0 At jct with busier rd → into shopping street 🍺 🛍 🍴 **Haarlemmerstraat**

27.5 After bridge immediately ← via 🚲 tunnel (to Central Station)

27.6 Immediately after tunnel ← via 🚲 bridge and ← via 🚲 on right-hand side of rd into tunnel

27.8 After tunnel cross rd 🚗🚗 at lhts and → via 🚲 on left-hand side of rd

28.0 Ferry landing Central Station (end of section 9)

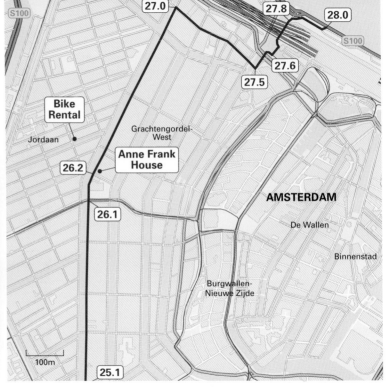

Section 10 (main): Amsterdam – Maarssen (39 km)

17th-century Amsterdam businessmen built their dream homes along the Vecht River. Most houses are still standing, defining the character of this idyllic river route.

Leaving Amsterdam is best along the busy Amsterdam-Rhine Canal where barges set off for their long journeys to Germany and beyond. The cycleway along this canal will carry you out of the urban sprawl, straight into the province of Utrecht, named after its capital city.

This is where you start travelling along the sleepy Vecht River. The merchants of the Dutch Golden Age built their country mansions and estates here and the route is therefore extremely scenic. The Vecht River has been an important inland trading route for centuries. In medieval times, forces of Holland and Utrecht regularly clashed in this area ("Vecht" literally means "fight" in Dutch). Various 17th-century country mansions along the river are built on foundations of older fortifications.

There are plenty of opportunities for breaks along the way, like at the pretty town of Weesp, the scenic village of Vreeland and the town of Breukelen ("Brooklyn" in English). It is not hard to guess that the New York district of Brooklyn is named after this Dutch town, so you could argue that the local river bridge in Breukelen can be called the original "Brooklyn Bridge". This section ends on the edge of the urban sprawl of Utrecht.

0.0 (= 42.2 or 28.0) At Amsterdam Central Station, go to main ferry landing and head east via 🚲 along water (to A'dam Oost/Almere & KP 5), keep going ↑ passing various jcts (to Zeeburg)

2.7 After office building "SBS" cross tram tracks and immediately ← via 🚲 (don't cross busy rd at jct!)

3.0 At jct with lhts → via 🚲 on right-hand side (C. van Eesterenlaan)

3.5 Just before T-jct ← via cobbled one-way rd, at end ↑ onto traffic-free 🚲 (Cruquiusweg; sign after 50 m)

3.5 For 🏠 Zeeburg leave route here, see map

4.1 At end of 🚲 ↗ onto rndabt, → via 🚲 on right-hand side (Th K. van Lohuizenlaan)

4.4 At T-jct ← via 🚲 on left-hand side

4.5 1st rd ↖, dead-end rd with speed bumps (Flevoparkweg, to Diemen/A'dam Zuidoost)

Leaving Amsterdam by bicycle is reasonably simple; it is only a couple of junctions with traffic lights to the start of the towpath route of the Amsterdam-Rhine Canal.

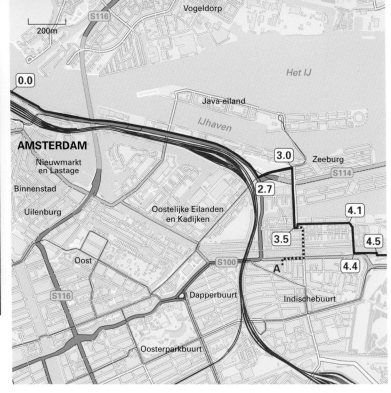

Section 10 (main): Amsterdam – Maarssen (39 km)

5.2 At rndabt → via canal rd (to Diemen/A'dam Zuidoost & KP 54), keep going ↑ along wide shipping canal for a long time, ignoring various 🚲 jcts

5.2 ⚓ **Amsterdam-Rhine Shipping Canal:** This 70 kilometre-long canal links the Amsterdam Docks with the Rhine River. The freight barges you see here might travel to/from Switzerland, France (via Mosel River) or even the Black Sea (via Danube River). Approx 50% of European inland freight shipping is operated by Dutch shipping companies. The Dutch fleet consists of approximately 7,500 barges. The Netherlands has over 1,400 kilometres of inland waterways suitable for large freight barges. This makes freight shipping a good alternative for road and rail; over 30% of all freight in The Netherlands is shipped.

11.8 On paved rd "Klein Merwede" (see sign) just before railway bridge → via traffic-free 🚲 (to Weesp/Hilversum), follow zigzag onto bridge

12.6 At end of bridge ↙ via 🚲 (to Muiden/Almere)

12.9 At T-jct ← via traffic-free 🚲 under bridge (Kanaalpad)

15.0 Where 🚲 ends at private gate ↖ via 🚲 on right-hand side of rd, go across bridge and follow zigzag

15.4 ⬅ 🛒 🎣 🍴 ⚓ **Weesp** Scenic town with various shops and cafés, 1 km away from main route; → at end of zigzag

15.4 At end of zigzag ← (to KP 42), 🚲 becomes rd

15.6 At T-jct ↗ via 🚲 on right-hand side under bridge, at end of 🚲 ← cross rd and immediately 1st rd → (to Nigtevecht/Loenen & KP 42)

16.3 At sharp bend to the left ↑ (to Nigtevecht/Loenen)

19.1 In Nigtevecht 🚲 ends, follow rd and opposite bus stop → (Raadhuisstraat, to Loenen/Utrecht), ↑

19.5 At jct with main rd ↟ via 🚲 on left-hand side

19.5 🪑 **Nigtevecht** (bench and picnic table at bridge)

19.6 After bridge 1st rd ← (Vreelandse Weg), keep going ↑ on country lane for a long time

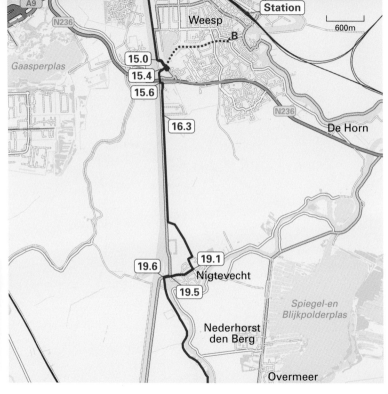

Section 10 (main): Amsterdam – Maarssen (39 km)

26.6 In Vreeland 1st rd ↖, one-way street with contra flow for cyclists (to Vreeland, Loenen)

26.9 At jct ↖ and immediately ← via historic bridge across river (to Loenen/Hilversum)

26.9 ⛴ 🏪 🛍 🍴 ⛲ **Vreeland** Pretty village; pancake restaurant and small shop

on street across the bridge

27.1 At jct with "stop" sign → (to Hilversum/Loenen), at end of rd ↑ via 🚲 (tunnel)

27.4 At end of tunnel ↗ (Boslaan, to Loenen & KP 25)

30.6 At jct with main rd (KP 25) ↑ via 🚲 crossing (to Nieuwersluis/Beukelen)

"Vreeland" literally means "peaceful land"; well it is!

32.2 In Nieuwersluis ↑ (to Breukelen/Utrecht)

32.2 ⚟ **Nieuwersluis** Benches on river side with views over bridge

35.2 ⚟ 🍴 👜 🍲 ⚟ 🍷 **Breukelen**
At KP 84 you can turn → across the river bridge into Breukelen town centre. You could regard this bridge as the original "Brooklyn Bridge". The town centre has various shops and eateries, but the most scenic part of town is around the bridge!

35.2 At bridge (KP 84) ↑ (to Maarssen/Utrecht & KP 46), keep going ↑

36.2 ⚟ **Nijenrode Castle**
Don't miss this largest country mansion along the Vecht River, located on the other riverbank. The building was originally a castle, dating from 1275. After being destroyed and rebuilt several times it became a stately home in 1675. Various rich families lived here until it became a business university in 1988.

39.0 👜 🍲 **Geesberge** (pub & terrace with river views)
39.0 End of section 10
- For the main route via Utrecht see section 11 (page 88)
- For the eastern route to Nijmegen see section 18 (page 126).

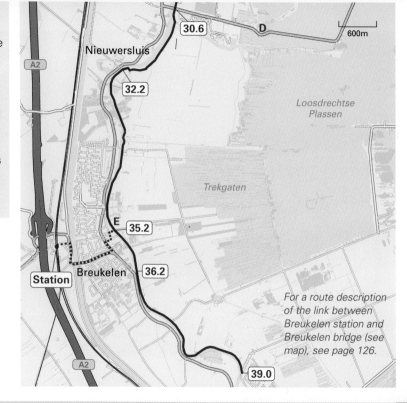

For a route description of the link between Breukelen station and Breukelen bridge (see map), see page 126.

Section 11 (main): Utrecht: Maarssen – De Haar (26 km)

Utrecht is the fourth largest city of The Netherlands and mostly unknown to international visitors. The marvel of Utrecht is its central Old Canal ("Oude Gracht"), without doubt the most scenic canal of the country. It is located on the historic course of the Vecht River and was created by damming the river at the city boundaries. This made it possible to lower the water level by approximately four metres, creating an inner-city harbour wharf system with storage cellars below street level. Most cellars have been transformed into restaurants, art galleries or offices.

The 112-metre-tall Dom Tower is Utrecht's other distinctive landmark. It is Europe's second highest cathedral tower (the highest being Cologne's in Germany) and was completed in 1382. The tower was separated from the cathedral during a fierce storm in 1674, making part of the cathedral collapse. A pavement pattern on the square in front of the tower shows the original size of the cathedral. It is 465 steps to the top of the tower and this climb is as close as you can get to a serious climbing adventure in The Netherlands! Guided tours start every hour and reservations are recommended (phone: +31 30 2360010). Buy your tickets next to the tower at the "RonDom"/Tourist Information "VVV" offices.

The beautiful Utrecht Old Canal – "Oude Gracht" – is probably the best kept secret of The Netherlands.

De Haar Castle is too heavy for its 1391 foundations, causing cracks in various walls of this majestic 1892 folly.

Utrecht is also a lively city. A large student population rules the place, so expect plenty of bars and restaurants with food being not too expensive. Utrecht is also a great place for shopping. Its central location attracts shoppers from all parts of the country. On the down side you have to know that the risk of bike theft in Utrecht is higher than anywhere else in The Netherlands. Ensure you use a guarded bike park (like "U-stal" at the town hall) or keep your bike(s) safe inside at your hotel/B&B.

You arrive in Utrecht by following the full course of the Vecht River. This river route keeps its peaceful character all the way from Maarssen to the locks at the start of the Old Canal, with one exception. The city of Utrecht has banned prostitutes from the city centre and "tolerates" in Dutch style a small red light district on the banks of the Vecht River, where prostitutes work on barges. It is safe to travel through so long as you don't take pictures!

The route leaving the city takes you past the majestic De Haar Castle, a hidden gem among ancient-looking parkland. Don't be fooled; all the beauty you see here was only created in 1892 on request by the rich Van Zuylen family. Folly or not, the building and surrounding park are gorgeous and extensive restoration is carried out to preserve the building for future generations.

Section 11 (main): Utrecht: Maarssen – De Haar (26 km)

0.0 (39.0) At pub "Geesberge" ↑ via river dyke rd

0.4 1st rd →, one-way street with contra flow for cyclists (to Centrum/Maarssenbroek & KP 46)

1.3 In shopping street 1st rd →, one-way street with contra flow for cyclists (Kaatsbaan, to KP 46)

1.3 ⁂ 🚉 🛒 🍴 ⚲ **Maarssen**

1.5 1st rd ← just before bridge (Langegracht, to Oud-Zuilen/ Utrecht)

1.8 At T-jct → via dead-end rd (to Oud-Zuilen/Utrecht)

1.9 Cross main rd ↑ via lhts (to Oud-Zuilen/Utrecht), keep going ↑ via river dyke rd

5.6 In Oud-Zuilen just before bridge ↖, keep Vecht River on right-hand side, ↑ via river dyke rd

5.6 ⁂ **Slot Zuylen Castle** Get a glimpse of this beautiful castle; ↖ via wide gravel path for 50 metres. Visits by guided tour only (starting every hour on weekend afternoons).

7.6 At jct of 3 rds → via dead river dyke rd (to KP 28)

8.4 At end of rd ↑ via 🚲 on left-hand side

8.4 ⁂ **Utrecht Canal Barges Red Light District** Caution: keep to the 🚲 and take extra care at rd crossings; no photography!

9.5 At T-jct ← (Jagerskade) and immediately → (Anthoniedijk), keep going ↑ at next 2 jcts

10.9 After passing some locks in the Vecht River (now a canal) at bend to the left ↑ via bridge (🚲 only)

10.9 ⇚ **Miffy Square ("Nijntje Pleintje")** Statue of this Utrecht-born children's character

10.9 At Miffy statue ↱ via bridge to other side of canal (Oude Gracht, LF 7a Oeverlandroute)

11.3 Dismount at main rd jct, walk ↑ into pedestrian zone (Oude Gracht), follow canal route

11.7 At small square next to the town hall (with the main canal underneath in a tunnel) 1st rd ← (Oudkerkhof), walk to next square (on left)

11.8 ⇚ 🏠 🛒 ☕ 🍴 🔧 **Utrecht (Town Hall)** Guarded bike park in town hall; see sign "U-stal"

11.8 To continue route resume cycling ↑ (Oudkerkhof)

11.9 At jct → (Domstraat)

12.0 At T-jct → (to KP 38), ↑ via cobbled rd with ⇚ **Utrecht Dom Tower** on your left-hand side

12.1 Follow cobbled rd around Dom Tower onto Servetstraat, then ↑ across "Oude Gracht" canal

12.3 At T-jct → via slightly wider rd, sharp bend to left

12.5 At major jct with lhts ↑ via 🚲 on right-hand side (LF 4b, Midden Nederland Route, sign across jct)

12.7 At bus station ↰ across tram tracks via 🚲 on left-hand side (LF 4b), follow 🚲 → around bus station

13.3 At end of 🚲 between bus and train stations 1st 🚲 ← via tunnel under railway (red tarmac)

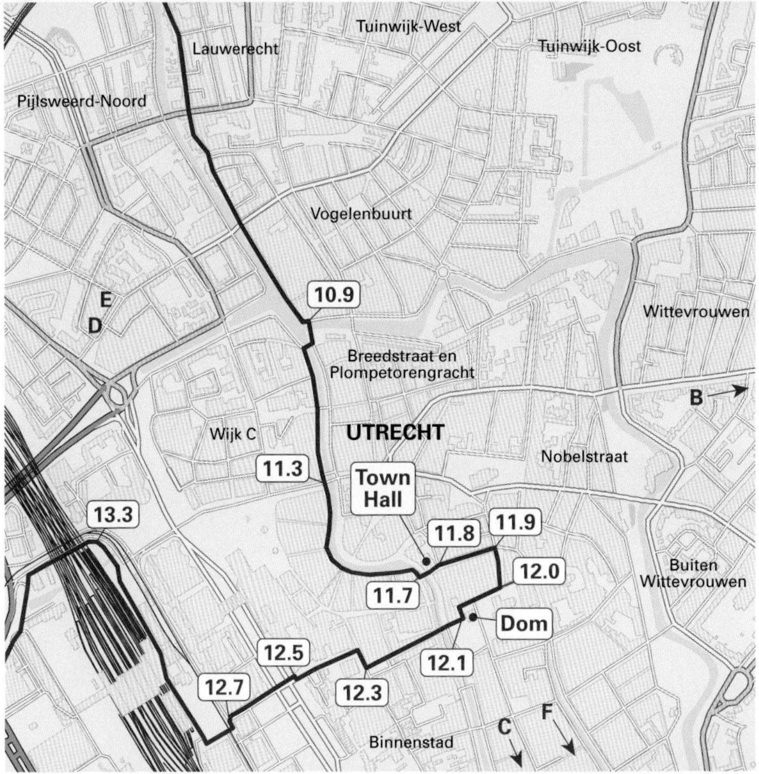

Section 11 (main): Utrecht: Maarssen – De Haar (26 km)

13.5 After railway tunnel ↑ at rd crossing, immediately ↖ via ᗱᖯ on left-hand side of main rd (with tram tracks in the middle, to Lombok/Vleuten)

13.6 At lhts → via ᗱᖯ crossing (to Lombok/Vleuten), at other side of main rd with tram tracks ← via ᗱᖯ crossing (to Dichterswijk/Kanaleneiland), then ↑ via ᗱᖯ feeding onto quiet canal rd

14.5 ↑ via ᗱᖯ bridge over canal and immediately → via ᗱᖯ along canal (to Lage Weide/Vleuten)

15.1 ← across bridge and immediately → via residential street (Kanaalweg)

15.4 At jct → via ᗱᖯ on right-hand side (to Lage Weide)

15.8 At major jct (church on corner) via ᗱᖯ crossing ← onto ᗱᖯ on right-hand side (to Terwijde/Vleuten)

16.0 Cross main rd ↑ via ᗱᖯ crossing (onto bridge "Amsterdam Rijn Kanaal", to Terwijde/Vleuten), keep following ᗱᖯ route to Terwijde/Vleuten through development area Leidsche Rijn/Terwijde.

The Netherlands is a very densely populated country. All the pleasant landscapes you have enjoyed so far can only be kept green by massive, dense building at allocated sites. "Leidsche Rijn" will be home to 80,000 people by 2015.

19.4 At train station "Utrecht Terwijde" → via lhts onto 🚲 under railway, after tunnel immediately ← via quiet rd with railway on left-hand side

20.3 After the very end of new housing estate 1st rd → (Enghlaan, to Utrecht & KP 13)

21.1 Country lane ends as 🚲 in new housing estate, here 1st rd ← and ↑ onto 🚲, bridge over main rd

21.9 After bridge via zigzags down ↑ via country lane

22.8 At jct with main rd ↑ via 🚲 on right-hand side (to Haarzuilens/Kockengen)

24.2 In Haarzuilens at KP 12 → via 🚲 on right-hand side (to Haarzuilens/Breukelen)

24.5 At far end of village green 1st rd ←, looping back

24.5 🚶 🍴 🍽 **Haarzuilens (village green and pub)** This village green is part of the 1892 folly "De Haar Castle". Haarzuilens village was completely rebuilt at expense of the castle owner. Note: most houses have window shutters bearing the castle shield.

24.6 At T-jct → (Brinkstraat), return in same direction where you came from

24.8 Pass village gate via 🚲 on left-hand side, at jct of KP 12 ↟ (to De Haar Castle, Harmelen & KP 11)

24.9 1st rd → (to Doorgaand Verkeer & KP 11)

25.7 🚶 🍴 🍽 **De Haar Castle** (end of section 11) Admission to the castle gardens € 3 pp; guided tours € 8 pp from the café in the castle basement

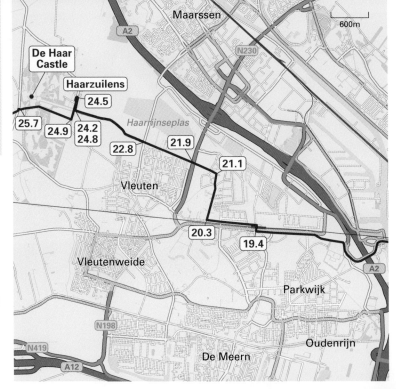

Section 12 (main): De Haar – Gouda (35 km)

From De Haar you will cycle into Holland's "Green Heart", a farmland belt of peace and quiet. Cycling is lovely along the curvy "Lange Linschoten" river where you also find a farm B&B with a canoe rental.

The town of Oudewater is home to the Witch Weighing Table Museum. Holy Roman Emperor Charles V (reign 1519-1556) was convinced that the Oudewater Weighing Table was the only "fair" equipment in his European empire to determine whether or not someone was a witch. It is possible to get your own weight checked, too!

Just before arriving in Gouda you have the opportunity to stock up on authentic Gouda cheese from some working Gouda cheese farms. Gouda itself has a pleasant medieval canal layout with a massive town square in the middle. This square has been the stage for the Gouda cheese market for centuries. The town council still puts on a traditional cheese market from mid-June until mid-August (Thursdays only, from 10 am until 12.30 pm). If you are able to make this you'll see farmers wearing traditional outfits and traditional trading. The scene takes place on the town square next to the "Waag", the original cheese-weighing house.

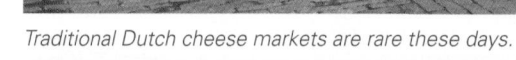

Traditional Dutch cheese markets are rare these days.

0.0 (= 25.7) Continue in western direction

0.1 At jct of KP 11 ← via 🚲 on right-hand side, then immediately → (Lagehaarse Dijk, to KP 10, LF 4b)

0.8 At end of rd at KP 10 → via traffic-free 🚲 (Kortjakse Pad, to KP 9)

1.7 At end of 🚲 at KP 9 ← (Gerverscop, to KP 73)

5.3 At T-jct at KP 73 ← via 🚲 on left-hand side (Leidsestraatweg, to KP 72 & 74)

5.4 1st rd →, across bridge → (Breeveld, to KP 72)

7.0 At KP 72 ↑ (to KP 71)

8.0 Just before main rd ↗ via 🚲 under bridge (to Kamerik/Centrum & KP 71)

8.1 After tunnel ↑ cross rd and immediately ↗ via narrow traffic-free 🚲 (towpath)

10.5 At end of towpath ← via 🚲 on left-hand side, at jct ↗ via 🚲 crossing to 🚲 at right-hand side, ↑ via 🚲 (to station & KP 69)

10.7 🚻 🍴 ⚡ **Woerden (Station)** Woerden is an old market town that has been extended massively since the 1970s to house Utrecht commuters. The town centre is 500 m away from the main route and has plenty of shops and cafés, offering plenty of opportunities for a break. It is good to know there are also some services at the station, directly on the route (in case you only want a very short break).

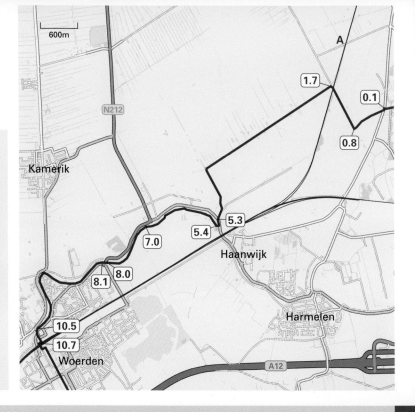

Section 12 (main): De Haar – Gouda (35 km)

10.7 At station → via traffic-free 🚲 route into tunnel under railway (to Linschoten/ Montfoort)

10.9 After tunnel ← (to Linschoten/Montfoort), follow bend to the right (to KP 60), keep going ↑ on traffic-calmed route (either rd or 🚲)

12.0 After cycling through 2 tunnels 1st rd → (Polaner Zandweg, to KP 69)

12.4 Follow route across bridge, then ← (Korte Linschoten W.Z., to KP 69)

12.8 After motorway viaduct at KP 69 2nd rd → (Haardijk, to KP 94), keep going ↑ until arrival in Snelrewaard

Modern development seems far away in the "Green Heart", where unspoilt farmland dominates the horizon.

19.6 In Snelrewaard at KP 94 ↑ (to KP 93)

20.0 At KP 93 ↑ (Kromme Haven, to Centrum & KP 92), keep canal on left-hand side

20.3 ‹ ⚑ 🍴 ⚲ 𝄞 **Oudewater** Small town with pleasant central square; there is a lively market on Wednesdays. On the central square you also find the witch weighing table museum "Heksenwaag". This small museum offers lots of fun for only a small entrance fee. Staff will invite you to be weighed on the original scales. If it can be proved you are not a witch you will receive an official certificate (closed on Mondays).

20.3 Continue ↑ via rd on right-hand side of canal (Peperstraat)

20.4 At jct ↑ (Wijdstraat, to Hekendorp/Haastrecht)

20.5 At church ↖ via narrow rd on left-hand side of church (Helletje), at canal ↗

20.7 At KP 92 ↑ via traffic-free 🚲, keep to low side of embankment (to Hekendorp/Haastrecht & KP 14)

21.2 At T-jct ↖ (to Hekendorp/Haastrecht)

25.0 At KP 14 ↑ (to Haastrecht/Gouda & KP 12), keep going ↑ via dyke rd (various small attractions on the high dyke rd, see next page)

25.1 ‹ ⚓ **Goejanverwellesluis** (pub and historic site, see next page)

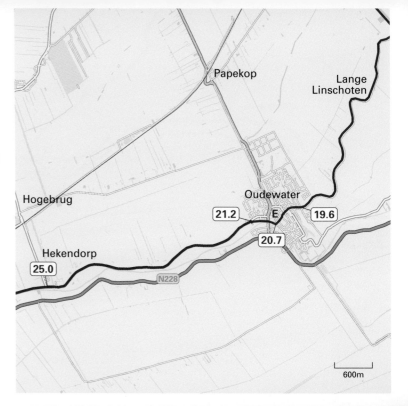

Section 12 (main): De Haar – Gouda (35 km)

25.0 The road over the high lock "Goejanverwellesluis" plays a significant role in Dutch history. Back in 1787, Dutch republicans (referring to themselves as "patriots") gained enough power to deny their King William V the control of the army and access to his royal palace in The Hague. The King decided to reside temporarily in the east of the country. This defeat was not taken lightly by his wife, Wilhelmina of Prussia, and she decided to head for The Hague. News about this journey spread fast and Gouda republicans stopped her entourage at the lock of Goejanverwellesluis. Wilhelmina was sent back east. Wilhelmina's brother (who was in charge of Prussia) was not pleased and came to his sister's aid. The Prussian army invaded and ended the republican revolt, reinstating William V (and Wilhelmina) in The Hague.

27.2 ⇷ 🐄 **Kaasboederij De Twee Hoeven** Buy authentic Gouda cheese direct from the farm!

28.3 At jct ↑ (Steinse Dijk, to Gouda), keep going ↑ via dyke route (either rd or 🚲)

28.8 ⇷ 🐄 **Kaasboederij 't Klooster:** Buy authentic Gouda cheese direct from the farm!

30.5 At jct ↑ (Goejanverwelledijk)

32.2 At T-jct ↖ via 🚲 on right-hand side

32.5 At 2nd jct with lhts ↗ via 🚲 on right-hand side of rd (to Centrum), join rd at end of 🚲, 🚗

32.8 At lhts ← via traffic-free 🚲 bridge (Doelenbrug), ↑ on rd (Doelenstraat)

33.0 1st rd → (Groeneweg)

33.1 1st rd → via car park (Koepoort) and immediately ← (Geuzenstraat)

33.3 At T-jct ← (to Markt, Langetiendeweg), dismount at bridge and walk ↑ into pedestrian zone

33.5 1st rd → (to Markt, Kortetiendeweg)

33.5 ⟨ 🏠 🚂 🛒 🍴 ⚓ **Gouda**

33.5 On arrival at central market square "Markt" ← and in corner ← (Wijdstraat), pedestrian zone

33.7 At jct ↗, ← to cross canal and immediately →, one-way street without contra flow for cyclists; dismount! (to "Hotel Keizerskroon")

33.9 2nd rd ← (Keizersstraat, to "Hotel Keizerskroon"), resume cycling, at hotel Keizerskroon ↑

34.1 At T-jct ← (to "De Mondriaan"), at next jct ↑ across bridge (Korte Noodgodsstraat)

34.3 At next jct before bridge → (Westhaven)

34.5 Dismount at T-jct with lhts and via pedestrian crossing ← via 🚲 on right-hand side (Nieuwe Veerstal, to Bergambacht/Reeuwwijk) 🚗

35.0 At jct → via 🚲 onto bridge (end of section 12)

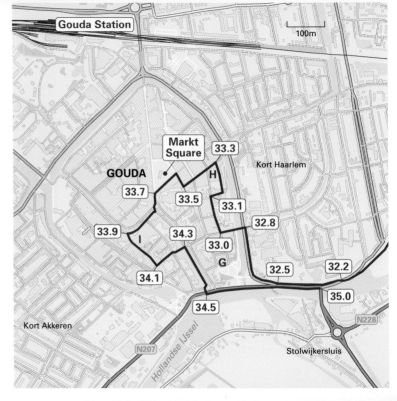

Section 13 (main): Gouda – Delft (44 km)

It is well worth spending some time in Delft.

From Gouda you cycle along the tidal Hollandse IJssel River towards Moordrecht. Between the Moordrecht and Zevenhuizen towns you cross Holland's lowest lands (22 feet below sea level) before arriving at some well-preserved windmills near the Rottemeren Lakes. This reserve borders the built-up area between The Hague and Rotterdam. For the next 10 kilometres or so you have to make your way through an area of greenhouses and housing estates. Near Delft the horizon widens and via a stretch through pleasant parkland you arrive in Delft.

Delft is well known for its pottery, with designs inspired by imported 17th-century Chinese porcelain. Delft also played an important role in Dutch history, as William of Orange (also known as William the Silent), leader of the Dutch revolt against Spanish rule, was murdered here. He is buried in the church on the main square, as are numerous generations of the Dutch royal family. Delft's best treasure is the charming medieval canal system; it is worth parking your bike at the guarded bike park and going for a stroll. The town centre is compact and you'll find all the attractions within a 10-minute walk (for more information, see page 103).

0.0 (= 35.0) Take 🚲 onto bridge (to Goudrak)

0.2 At rndabt → via dyke rd (to Goudrak) 🚗

4.6 In Goudrak at sign for ferry to Moordrecht → to ferry landing (charge ferry € 0.80 pp, cash only)

4.7 🚉 **Moordrecht**

4.7 Across ferry ↑ cross dyke rd, in front of church ↖, one-way street with cyclists contra flow (Kerkplein)

5.0 At jct ↗ (Kerklaan, to Rotterdam/Den Haag) 🚗, after bridge use 🚲 on right-hand side

5.3 At jct via 🚲 crossings ↑ to 🚲 on left-hand side (to Rotterdam/Den Haag), keep following this 🚲

6.8 At railway level crossing ↑ via 🚲 on left-hand side (to Nieuwerkerk/Rotterdam)

7.1 After motorway viaduct with slip roads 1st 🚲 ↖ and immediately ← via rd with poor surface

8.3 ⬿ **Holland's lowest lands** This area, "Zuidplaspolder", is the lowest point of The Netherlands. These fields are 6.75 metres (22 feet) below general North Sea high tide level. During big storms, sea levels can rise 3 to 4 metres above this level, so in the event of a flood the gantries on the motorway on your left would be completely covered by water! All Dutch sea defences can cope with sea levels up to 5 metres higher than normal and should be able to withstand waves of 7 metres high on top of that.

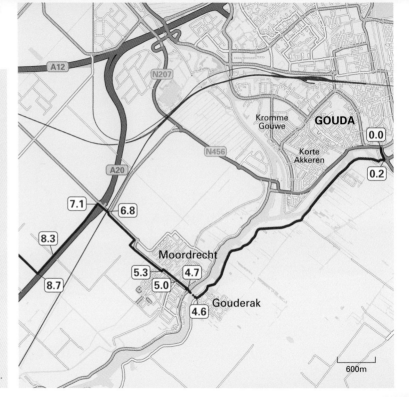

Section 13 (main): Gouda – Delft (44 km)

8.7 1st tarmac rd → (Derde Tochtweg)

12.7 In Zevenhuizen at give way jct ← via 🚲 on left-hand side of rd, at end of 🚲 join rd 🚗

13.4 At jct with lhts ↑ (to Centrum)

13.5 At next jct → (Dorpsstraat, to Moerkapelle), keep going ↑ via this rd

13.9 🚉 🍴 ⚡ **Zevenhuizen** Nondescript town with modest high street

15.3 Just before end of rd ↑ via 🚲 on left-hand side

15.4 1st rd ← (Molenweg, to "Molenviergang")

15.5 1st rd ↖ (to "Molenviergang")

16.8 At T-jct ↑ cross bridge and → via traffic-free 🚲 (to Zoetermeer/Den Haag)

17.7 ↙ 🏚 **Windmills Zevenhuizen:** You can clearly see here how every individual windmill scoops the water from a lower canal about a metre up to a higher canal. A line of windmills can bring the water up 4 to 6 metres. You'll find a picnic area beyond the bridge across the main canal.

17.7 After bridge and picnic area ← via traffic-free 🚲 (to Bleiswijk/Rotterdam)

19.6 At next jct ↑ via "fietspad" (to Rotterdam)

19.6 🍴 **Nesselande café**

21.6 At next jct → (to Bleiswijk)

22.0 Just before rndabt ↟ via 🚲, cross rd ↑ via 🚲 on left-hand side (to Bleiswijk), follow 🚲 to end

23.5 At end of 🚲 ← via 🚲 on right-hand side of rd (to "andere richtingen"), cross main rd via 🚲 lhts and ← (Overbuurtse Weg, to Bergschenhoek)

23.8 1st rd → (dead-end rd to "Berkel & Rodenrijs")

25.2 At end of rd ← via traffic-free 🚲 (to Bergschenhoek)

26.3 At jct (rd under construction) ↑ via traffic-free 🚲

27.2 At next jct ← via 🚲 on right-hand side, at rndabt ↗ via tarmac rd (to Berkel & Rodenrijs/Pijnacker)

27.7 After bend to the right and bridge immediately ← via traffic-free 🚲 (no signs, paved surface)

28.0 At next rd jct → into "Berkel & Rodenrijs"

28.2 At bend to the right ↖ (Van der Hoevenlaan)

28.3 At T-jct → (Johan van Oldenbarneveltlaan), at next T-jct ←

28.5 At jct with lhts ← (Rodenrijseweg) 🚗

28.8 At busy rndabt via 🚲 crossings ↑ 🚗

30.6 ⛽ **Berkel & Rodenrijs** (petrol station only)

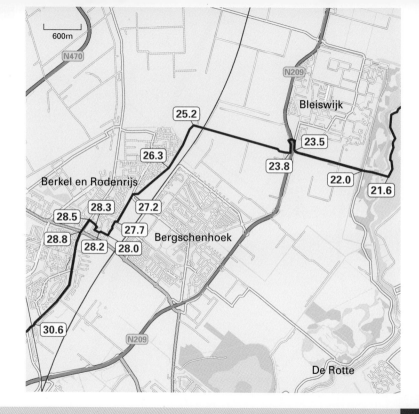

Section 13 (main): Gouda – Delft (44 km)

30.6 Join 🚲 on right-hand side ↗, at 🚲 jct immediately ↖ via 🚲 tunnel under railway

30.8 At next jct cross rd ↑ via 🚲 crossing, then immediately ↗, continue on rd with canal on right-hand side (Rodenrijseweg)

32.6 At T-jct → (to Delft/ Delftgauw)

32.8 At next jct ↑ via dyke rd (dead-end rd to Oude Leede/ Pijnacker, becomes "fietspad" later)

33.3 After bridge immediately ← via traffic-free 🚲 (narrow gravel path)

35.5 Just before motorway ↑ via rd tunnel (to Zweth/ Schiedam)

35.6 After tunnel ↑ via tarmac traffic-free 🚲 route (to Zweth/Schiedam), ↑ to end of path

36.4 At T-jct → via 🚲 on right-hand side, passing under high cycle bridge (to Delft), keep going ↑

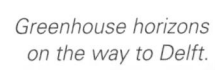

Greenhouse horizons on the way to Delft.

41.2 Where rd bends to the right cross rd ↖ via 🚲 crossing and ↗ via residential street (no sign)

41.7 At end of rd → (Kanaalweg, to Centrum)

41.8 1st bridge ← cross canal and follow 🚲 into tunnel

41.9 ⋐ 🏠 🖼 📷 🍴 ⚡ **Delft**
Guarded bike park at Vesteplein. Things to do:
- Enjoy "Markt" square. Dutch royals find their last resting place in the Nieuwe Kerk (New Church).
- See real Delftware pottery at Aardewerkatelier de Candelaer, just off "Markt"

square on Kerkstraat.
- See the bullet hole in the wall where William the Silent was assassinated in Prinsenhof Museum (admission € 3 pp); near Oude Kerk (Old Church).
- Take a scenic canal boat tour. Departs from Koornmarkt canal, just south of the "Markt" Square.

41.9 From tunnel, continue via 🚲, cross canal bridge, then immediately ← (to "Doorgaand Verkeer")

42.1 At T-jct ← via narrow 🚲 on right-hand side, ↗ via 🚲 lane (to Den Ham/Schipluiden) 🚗🚗

42.2 At lths → (to Station/Nootdorp) via 🚲 lane 🚗🚗

42.5 At jct with lhts ← via 🚲

crossings (to Station), after bridge immediately → (Houttuinen)

42.8 After tunnel under railway ↑ via one-way street with contra flow for cyclists (Buitenwatersloot, to Den Hoorn/Naaldwijk), keep going ↑

43.6 🚲 bridge over canal (end of section 13)

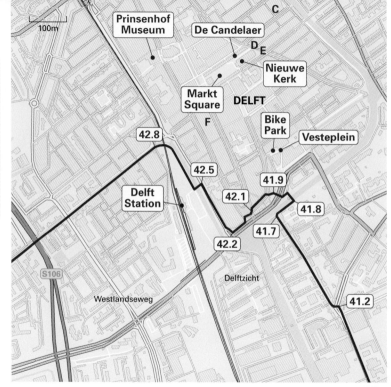

Section 14 (main): Delft – Hook of Holland (20 km)

Beyond Delft, the horizon is mostly taken over by greenhouse developments. This area is known as "De glazen stad" ("the city of glass") and not without reason! These greenhouses stretch for miles and miles and are responsible for a massive multi-million Euro all-year-round produce of flowers, plants, fruit and vegetables. It is very likely that products from this area find their way to your home via your local garden centre or supermarket.

On the way to Hook of Holland you not only cycle on various farm roads in between the greenhouses, but also on designated cycle routes through some pleasant stretches of parkland, like the "Staalduyn" area.

Schipluiden is a pretty village in a small area of open polder land. This place is surrounded by the urban developments of The Hague, Delft and Rotterdam. It is an important archaeological site with a settlement dating from 3000 BC, the oldest known in The Netherlands.

Just before arriving in Hook of Holland you can choose to visit the impressive Rotterdam storm surge barrier "Maeslantkering". The barrier is two miles away from the main route and is well worth a visit, see also page 42.

A look inside a Dutch trading centre; about 50% of the greenhouse produce consists of flowers and plants, the other 50% fruit and vegetables.

0.0 (43.6) Via 🚲 bridge ↑ to other side of canal (to Den Ham/Naaldwijk), keep going ↑

1.1 In Den Hoorn at jct ↑ (to Naaldwijk/De Lier)

1.3 🅿 🍴 **Den Hoorn** (Snack bar "De Pitstop")

1.3 At jct with eatery (KP 53) ↖, keep the canal on your left-hand side (to Sportcomplex Den Hoorn)

1.5 1st bridge ← across canal (to Delft/Schiedam) and immediately → (to KP 56), keep going ↑

3.4 At split of 🚲 ↗ via 🚲 staying close to canal on right-hand side

3.6 Cross rd ↑ via traffic-free 🚲

3.9 At T-jct (KP 56) →, after bridge ← (to Maasland/Maassluis & KP 55) 🚗

3.9 ♿ 🅿 **Schipluiden**

4.4 At T-jct ← (to KP 55) and immediately → via traffic-free 🚲 (to 't Woudt & KP 55)

5.3 At KP 55 ↑ onto bridge over canal (to KP 32)

6.6 At 2nd sharp bend to the right ↑ via traffic-free 🚲 (to KP 32)

7.2 At 🚲 T-jct (KP 32) ↑ via traffic-free 🚲 (to KP 31)

7.3 At rd jct → via tarmac rd (ignore sign to KP 31)

7.5 At jct ↙ via rd leading to some houses (no signs), keep going ↑ at various jcts (rd is named Burgerdijkseweg at first, later Oudecampsweg)

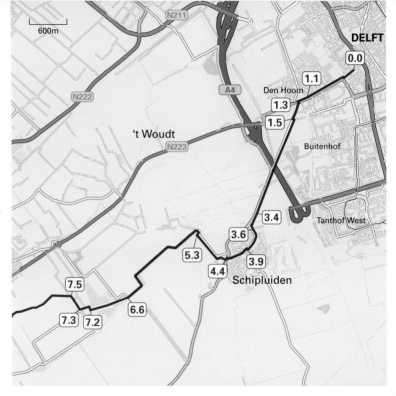

Section 14 (main): Delft – Hook of Holland (20 km)

10.2 At KP 29 → via tarmac rd (Hoefweg, to KP 25)

11.4 In Westerlee at T-jct ← (Leehove)

11.7 2nd rd → (Leeweg)

11.9 On sharp bend to the left ↑ via ᨆ on left-hand side of one-way rd, follow this ᨆ to end

12.0 ⛽ **Westerlee** (petrol station only)

12.2 At jct with lhts → via 1st ᨆ crossing, then immediately ← via 2nd ᨆ crossing (to Maasdijk), then ↑ across bus lanes and ↖ via ᨆ on right-hand side (to Maasdijk/Hoek van Holland)

12.7 Cross rd ↑ to ᨆ on left-hand side

13.2 At jct with lhts ↑ via ᨆ crossing, then immediately → via ᨆ crossing without lhts onto parallel rd

13.5 After bridge 1st rd ← (to Staelduyn/Hoek van Holland & KP 23)

14.5 At KP 23 → via ᨆ on left-hand side (Bonnenlaan, to KP 18)

15.3 🏕 **Staelduyn picnic area**

16.1 At KP 18 ↑ via traffic-free 🚲 (to Hoek van Holland & KP 19)

17.3 At end of 🚲 (KP 19) ← via 🚲 on left-hand side (Haakweg, to Hoek van Holland-Centrum/Harwich & KP 22), 🚲 moves later to right-hand side of rd

18.4 At jct ↑ via 🚲 on right-hand side of rd (to Maeslantkering & KP 22, ignore signs for Hoek van Holland at this jct!)

18.5 ⚡ **Storm surge barrier Maeslantkering** To visit this barrier (see also page 42) ↑ at KP 22, after railway level crossing ← at T-jct, 1st rd →, keep going along canal for 2 kilometres.

18.5 For main route at KP 22 ↗ via traffic-free 🚲 on top of dyke (to Station/Harwich & KP 21)

19.6 At 🚲 jct ↖ via traffic-free 🚲 (to Station Haven/Harwich & KP 21)

20.2 Dismount at zebra crossing, ← via footpath across railway tracks to the Stenaline ferry terminal (end of section 14)

- If you started your journey from Europoort with your own bikes, you'll need section 2 again to return to the ferry terminal (see page 41)
- If you started your journey from IJmuiden or Amsterdam, continue reading at section 3 to continue the circular route (see page 42).

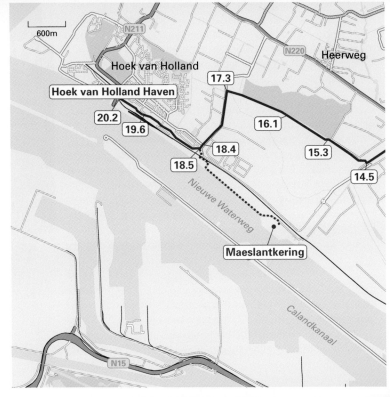

Section 15 (northern): Amsterdam – Volendam (21 or 30 km)

Have your picture taken in traditional Volendam costume or watch a Dutch football match in style in a Volendam pub.

This section is probably the most "Dutch" route of all. You'll cycle mostly on the former Zuiderzee seawall, providing splendid views of Lake IJsselmeer. Scenic dyke villages like Nieuwendam, Durgerdam and Uitdam are utterly charming, but it is the peninsula of Marken and bustling Volendam you definitely don't want to miss.

Marken represents the natural history of The Netherlands as no other place in the country. It was once part of the mainland, but medieval floods transformed the area into an island in the Zuiderzee. Only after the Zuiderzee was turned into an inland lake did the regular flooding come to an end. Traditional houses on high wooden pillars are a reminder of the wind and waterswept past. You'll reach Marken via the 1957 causeway. Have a good stroll around before boarding the pedestrian ferry to Volendam, as Marken is one of the few Dutch places where you might run into a local in authentic traditional costume!

Volendam has plenty of traditional costumes as well, but these exist entirely to dress up tourists. This former thriving fishing village is on the itinerary of all coach trips from Amsterdam and not without reason. Its harbour is extremely scenic and thanks to the tourists, full of life!

0.0 Take ferry to IJplein from landing behind Amsterdam Central Station

0.0 At IJplein landing ↑ via 🚲 to Vliegenbos, later 🚲 on right-hand side (Meeuwenlaan)

1.4 After rndabt at 2nd bus shelter "Merelstraat" → via traffic-free 🚲 into park

2.4 ⇇ 🚲 **Nieuwendam** (café "'t Sluisje") Nieuwendam is an old village situated on the former sea wall of the IJ-bay. This wide stretch of water is now mostly reclaimed, as you can see on your right. The lock was mostly used by farmers, who transported their produce (mainly dairy) to Amsterdam via small barges.

2.9 At jct ↑ via dyke ridge route (to Schellingwoude)

3.4 At rd crossing ↑ via 🚲 (to Schellingwoude)

3.6 After next rd crossing immediately ↗ via 🚲 onto rd on dyke ridge and ↑ (to Schellingwoude)

(via iron gate)

1.7 After entrance ⚠ Vliegenbos at jct ↖ via main 🚲

1.9 1st 🚲 ← via bridge and ← via rd (Schellingwoude Route)

2.0 At T-jct → (Nieuwendammerdijk, Schellingwoude Route)

4.7 At jct ↑ via rd with dyke ridge on right-hand side (to Durgerdam), later join 🚲 on left-hand side

5.2 At KP 46 ↑ 🚲 on left-hand side (to Durgerdam & KP 45, LF 21a Zuiderzee Route)

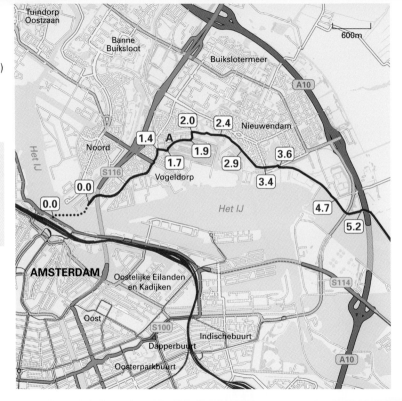

Section 15 (northern): Amsterdam – Volendam (21 or 30 km)

6.4 At end of 🚲 via rd ↑
into Durgerdam

6.8 ↲ 🚢 🍽 **Durgerdam** ("De
Oude Taveerne")

7.8 At end of village at jct (KP
47) ↗ via traffic-free 🚲 onto
dyke ridge (Zuiderzeepad, to
Enkhuizen), keep following
🚲 on dyke ridge

*Don't miss out on the pedestrian ferry to Volendam from Marken Harbour to have
the full IJsselmeer experience!*

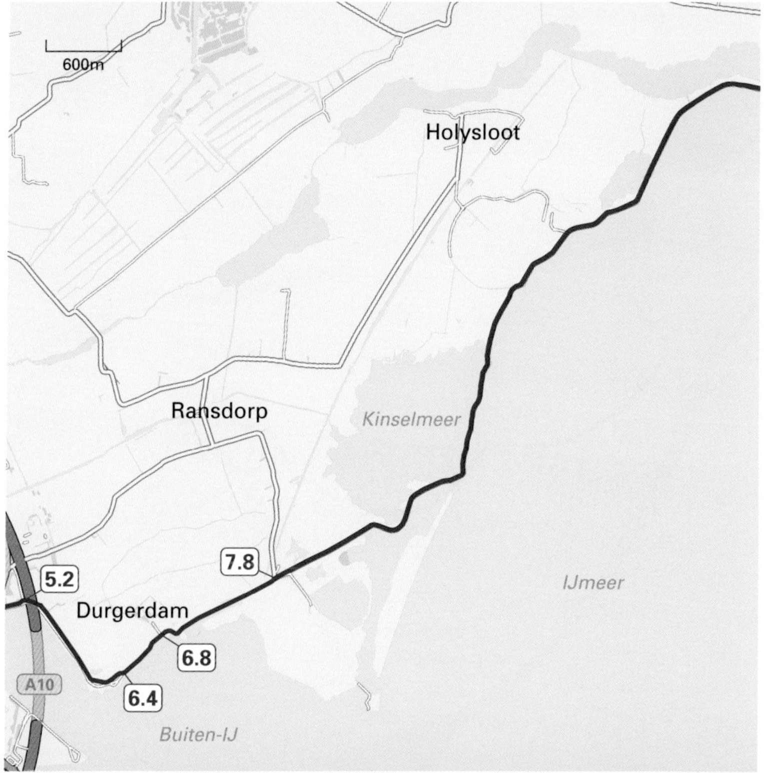

14.8 At end of 🚲 via rd ↑
into Uitdam

15.2 At jct (KP 77) ↑ (to Marken
& KP 52), when leaving
village ↗ via "fietspad"
onto dyke ridge

16.0 Ep ↗ via rd (to Marken), after
entrance ⛺ 🛏 🍴 Uitdam ↗
via "fietspad" (to KP 52)

17.3 At jct cross rd ↑ to 🚲 at
other side (KP 52)
🪑 **Gouwzee** (picnic area on
right)

- Here you have to choose
between the main route via
Marken and ferry
to Volendam (€ 6 pp
including bike, ferry
operates until 5 pm, Easter-
Oct). Alternatively you can
use the (longer) route via
Monnickendam, which
bypasses Marken island.

Main route via Marken/ferry:

17.3 → via 🚲 on left-hand side
(to Marken & KP 51)

19.7 At end of causeway
immediately ← via
"fietspad", paved path
on old dyke ridge

20.9 Ep → follow path
around harbour

21.0 🚏 🏠 🛏 🍴 **Marken**

21.0 Opposite "Seitje Boes
Souvenirs" ← onto quay
for pedestrian ferry to
Volendam ("bootvaart
Marken-Volendam"),
end of section 15

**Alternative route via
Monnickendam:**

17.3 ← via 🚲 on right-hand side
(to Monnickendam)

20.4 Ep cross rd ↑ to continue
via 🚲 on left-hand side
(to "Doorgaand Verkeer
& KP 55, LF 21a) (continued
on page 113)

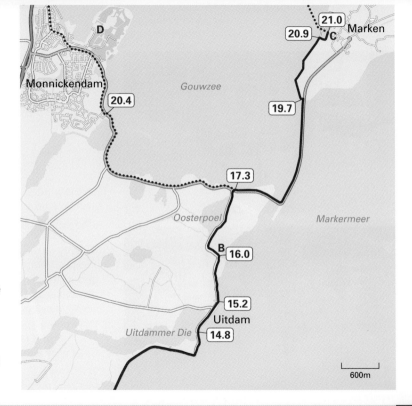

Section 16 (northern): Volendam – Hoorn (25 km)

From Volendam it is only a stone's throw to Edam. The weekly Edam cheese market was installed during the 16th century and you can't pass through Edam without having a quick look at the small cheese exhibition in the old weighing house, "De Waag". More Edam history is available in the "Edams Museum" in the town hall on the main square (admission € 3 pp).

From Edam the route temporarily heads inland via peaceful farmland. The village of Middelie mostly consists of one road with farms scattered along it. Oosthuizen is a bigger place with some local shops. From there you'll head back to the IJsselmeer coast.

Via tiny Schardam you'll make your way to Hoorn. Hoorn's port used to equal Amsterdam's in importance during the Dutch Golden Age. The city has many fine historic buildings and one of the longest shopping streets in The Netherlands. It is well worth spending some time here before heading on to Enkhuizen. This is a longer ride, entirely on the ridge of the former Zuiderzee seawall. Of course, you'll get great views over the IJsselmeer here, but stock up on provisions in Hoorn as there is not much out there until you arrive in Enkhuizen.

(Top) The splendid main watch tower of Hoorn reflects the city's wealth during the Dutch Golden Age. (Below) Edam's town hall is more modest, but still pretty as well.

Note: route Volendam-Hoorn starts on next page!

Alternative route via Monnickendam (continued):

21.8 At rndabt → onto rd via ⟢ crossing (Zuideinde, to Volendam)

21.9 At jct ↑ via one-way rd with contra flow for cyclists (Zuideinde, to Volendam)

22.2 ⟨ ▲ ⛽ ⟢ 🍴 ⚲ **Monnickendam**

22.2 At bridge over old lock ↑, at next jct ↗ (Noordeinde, to "Alle richtingen", LF21a)

22.7 At KP 56 cross bridge ↑ (to Katwoude & KP 99, LF 21a), join ⟢ on right-hand side after 100 m

23.2 At lhts → via rd (to Katwoude & KP 99)

23.2 ⟨ ⛽ **Irenehoeve** (cheese and clogs farm shop)

23.5 ⟢ 🍴 **De Zeilhoek** (restaurant overlooking lake)

23.8 ⟨ ⛽ **Henri Willig** (cheese farm shop)

28.4 At jct → via ⟢ on right-hand side (to Volendam & KP 99, LF 21a Zuiderzee Route)

28.6 Ep ↑ via rd onto dyke ridge and ↑ via ⟢ on ridge

28.8 ⟢ 🍴 **Marina Volendam**

28.8 Ep ↑ via dyke route (to Haven, LF 21a Zuiderzeeroute)

29.8 ⟨ 🏠 ⛽ ⟢ 🍴 ⚲ **Volendam** Historic harbour, ferry landing "Marken Express"; end of alternative route via Monnickendam

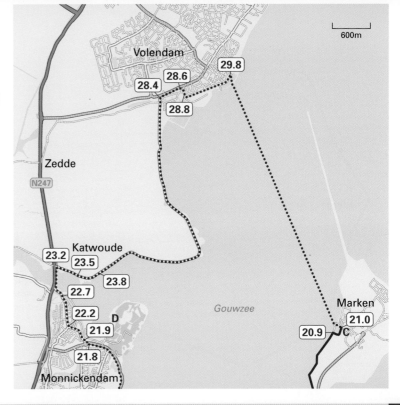

Section 16 (northern): Volendam – Hoorn (25 km)

0.0 (= 21.0 or 29.8) Coming from ferry landing "Marken Express" → via dyke rd (go in between "Café De Boer" and "Cathrien Brasserie"

1.0 At end of historic town ↑ via lower rd (with dyke ridge on right-hand side of rd)

1.5 At T-jct → to KP 97, later ↑ at historic sea locks

3.9 1st rd → via 2 bridges (to Warder & KP 97)

4.0 After 2nd bridge at KP 97 ← (Voorhaven, to Centrum & KP 95)

4.7 ⚐ ⌂ 🛏 📷 🍴 **Edam** (high bridge over canal)

4.8 At jct ↑ (Kleine Kerkstraat, to KP 95, LF 21b)

5.0 At jct follow rd → (Lingerzijde, to KP 95)

Traditional means of transporting Edam cheese.

5.1 At sharp bend to left ↖ via 🚲 tunnel (to KP 95)

5.2 After tunnel cross rd ↑ at KP 95 (Groot Westerbuiten, to Middelie & KP 94)

5.4 Just before bridge 2nd rd → (Zeevangsdijkje, to Middelie & KP 93)

7.0 1st rd ↗ (Buitengouwweg, lined with trees)

8.0 🏠 🛏 🍴 **Middelie** (hotel after 200 m; ← at jct)

8.0 At jct ↑ (Middelie, to Oosthuizen)

9.7 🎪 at jct

9.7 At jct ↑ (Middelie, to Oosthuizen & KP 11)

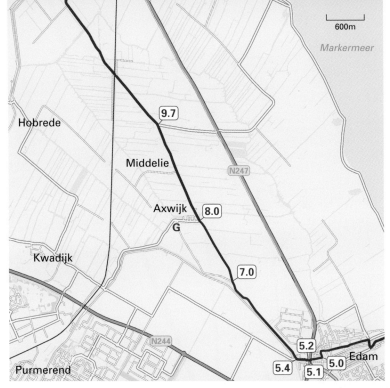

Section 16 (northern): Volendam – Hoorn (25 km)

12.0 At KP 11 ↑ (to KP 10), keep going ↑

13.3 At T-jct → (to Oosthuizen & KP 10)

13.4 At jct ↑ via one-way rd with contra flow for cyclists (to Oosthuizen & KP 10)

13.7 🚲 Oosthuizen

14.0 Cross main rd 🚗🚗 ↑ (Oosteinde, to Warder)

14.2 At jct ↑ (Oosteinde, to Schardam)

14.3 🛏 🍴 **Café Restaurant Ans & Piet**

14.3 ↑ at level crossing

16.0 At T-jct ← (IJsselmeerdijk, to Hoorn & KP 83, LF 21a Zuiderzeeroute), keep going ↑

17.4 At KP 83 ↑ (to Hoorn & KP 37, LF 21a)

18.5 At KP 37 1st rd → (to Hoorn & KP 36, LF 21a)

In Schardam you'll find this obelisk, also known as a "banpaal". These kinds of obelisks used to define the borders of influence of city courts. Beyond this obelisk the court of Hoorn used to be in charge.

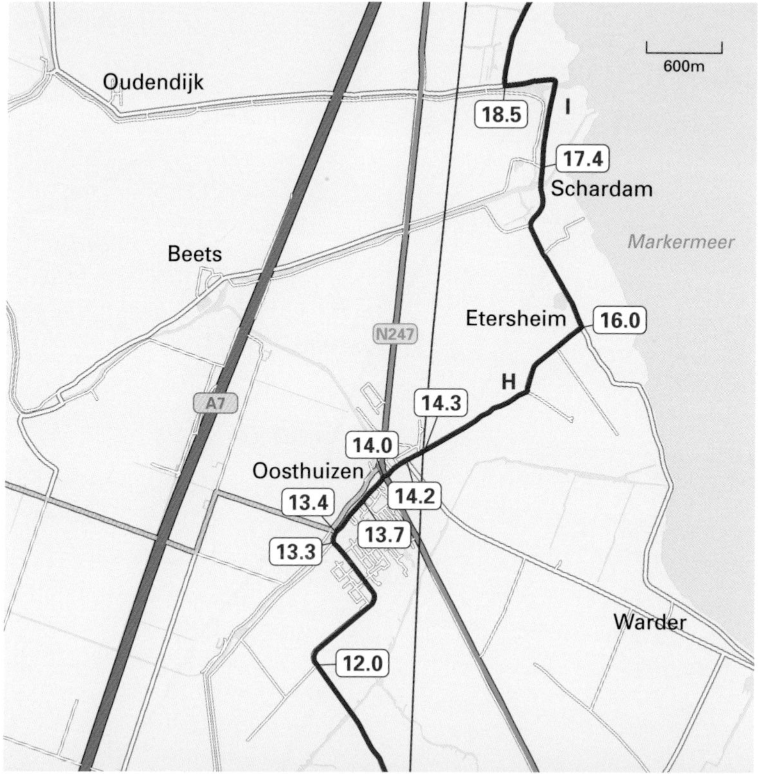

600m

Oudendijk

18.5 | I

17.4

Schardam

Markermeer

Beets

Etersheim 16.0

N247

H

A7 14.3

14.0

Oosthuizen 14.2

13.4 13.7

13.3

12.0

Warder

19.5 ⬅ **Monument Bedijkte Waal**
(views over lake)

20.4 🍴 **Ootje Konkel**
(pancake restaurant)

21.0 At KP 36 ↑ (to Hoorn &
KP 58, LF 21a)

22.4 At KP 58 ↑ (to Hoorn &
KP 59, LF 21a) 🚗

24.8 At jct ↑ via shopping street
with contra flow for cyclists
(LF 21a Zuiderzeeroute) 🚗

Things to see and do in Hoorn:
- Enjoy the historic harbour with Hoorn's landmark, the 1532 main watch tower. At its base you also find a small statue of three boys, known as the "sailor boys of Bontekoe", honouring a well-known children's book based on the original skipper's journals from the 17th century. Also see the East India Trading Company warehouses on Bierkade (like "Londen" and "Dantzig"). The Museum of the 20th century (also on Bierkade) houses a miniature display of Hoorn as it was in 1650.
- For a real catch-up on Hoorn's rich history, go to the "Westfries Museum" on the main square (east end of shopping area). The collection consists of paintings and various artifacts found in the Hoorn area. Of course there are also displays about the East India Trading Company VOC and about the life of Willem Corneliszoon Schouten, the man who named Cape Horn (southern tip of South America) after his hometown (admission € 8 pp).

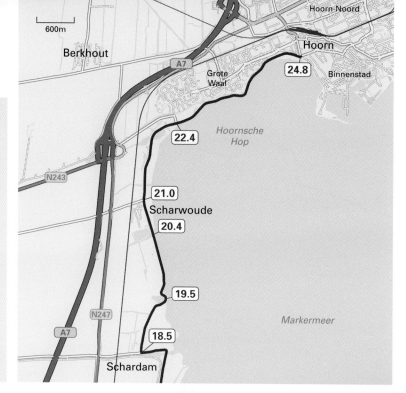

Section 17 (northern): Hoorn – Enkhuizen (28 km)

0.0 (=24.9) 1st rd → via one-way rd with contra flow for cyclists (Achterom, LF 21a Zuiderzeeroute) 🚗

0.5 At bend to right ← via alleyway "fietspad" (Proostensteeg, LF 21a Zuiderzeeroute)

0.6 ⚐ ⌂ 🚻 📷 🍴 ℹ **Hoorn** (central square & shopping)

0.6 At square ↗ (Grote Oost, to KP 62, LF 21a)

0.8 1st rd → (Wijdebrugsteeg, LF 21a)

1.0 ⚐ 📷 🍴 **Hoorn** (historic harbour and tower)

1.0 At T-jct ← (Oude Doelenkade, to KP 62, LF 21a)

1.3 At jct → via bridge (to "Alle richtingen", to KP 62)

1.6 At jct ↑ via 🚲 on right-hand side, leading onto traffic-free 🚲 on dyke ridge (Schellinkhoutdijk, LF 21a Zuiderzeeroute), follow dyke ridge route

Hoorn-Noord

Hoorn Station

Venenlaankwartier

A

0.0 B

D

Hoorn

Hoornsche Hop

Westfries Museum

1.3 C

1.6

0.8

0.6

0.5

Binnenstad

1.0

Tower

100m

Markermeer

3.1 At rd crossing ↑ via dyke ridge route (to KP 62, LF21a Zuiderzeeroute)

5.8 At KP 62 ↑ via dyke ridge route (to KP 80, LF21a Zuiderzeeroute), keep going ↑ via dyke ridge route

6.1 ☛ **Schellinkhout** (crazy golf café "Midget")

The IJsselmeerdijk between Hoorn and Enkhuizen.

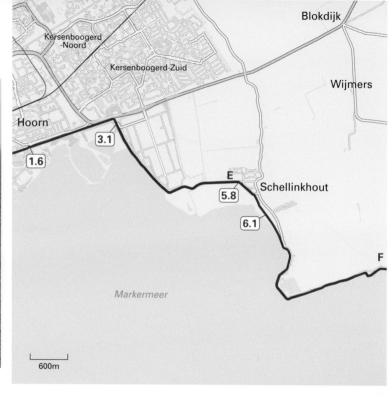

Section 17 (northern): Hoorn – Enkhuizen (28 km)

Enkhuizen has a similar history to Hoorn. It was an important port during the Dutch Golden Age and was a stronghold for the Dutch East India Trading Company. Fishing also brought the city wealth; Enkhuizen used to have the biggest herring fleet in the country. Enkhuizen is unique in the way that its medieval street and canal pattern has survived intact including the fortified embankments and walls around the city. This is why the route almost completely circumnavigates the whole town before making its way to the harbour and train station.

A visit to Enkhuizen is not complete without visiting the Zuiderzee Museum. This is the place to find out about life on the shores of this former Dutch sea bay, which brought both fortune and misery (floods) for centuries. The open-air museum has a fine collection of historic buildings (like a steam-powered launderette) and shows traditional ways of smoking fish, making sails, etc. The inner museum building has a fine collection of historic ships and an excellent display of the Zuiderzee works that turned the bay into a freshwater lake, and nearly half of it into newly reclaimed land. This is a full day out and also includes a boat tour. Admission is € 14 pp (multiple entries); English language information available.

Venhuizen

De Weed

Wijmers

Oosterleek

Wijdenes

Markermeer

600m

20.0 At near end of dyke ridge route (rndabt main rd ahead) ↗ via dead-end rd on dyke ridge (to KP 28, LF 21a Zuiderzeeroute)

20.3 At end of rd → via 🚲 on right-hand side (to KP 28, LF 21a Zuiderzeeroute)

20.6 At KP 28 1st 🚲 → to tunnel (to KP 27, LF 21a)

20.8 After tunnel 1st path →, dismount and walk bikes (Kleine Kaai, to KP 27, LF 21a Zuiderzeeroute)

20.9 Cross locks ↑ and resume cycling on paved rd, later tarmac, keep going ↑

20.9 ⟵ 📷 🍴 **Broekerhaven** (historic harbour)

21.7 At jct with windmill on left ↑ to level crossing (Broekerhavenweg, to Enkhuizen, LF 21a) 🚗

22.1 At T-jct (KP 27) → (Hoofdstraat, to Enkhuizen & KP 30, LF 21a Zuiderzeeroute) 🚗

Steam-powered launderette in Zuiderzeemuseum Enkhuizen.

Lutjebroek
Grootebroek
Bovenkarspel
Broekerhaven
Oostergouw
Venhuizen
Markermeer

N302

600m

Section 17 (northern): Hoorn – Enkhuizen (and beyond) (28 km)

23.6 At jct with lhts ↑ via 🚲 crossing (to Centrum & KP 30, LF 21a Zuiderzeeroute) 🚗

23.9 Immediately after historic gate ← (Nassaustraat) and immediately ↖ via "fietspad" onto embankment (Drechterlandroute)

25.4 At end of embankment route cross rd ↑ via one-way rd with cyclists contra flow (to KP 30)

25.5 Immediately after bend to right ← via 🚲 (Donkere Laantje, Drechterlandroute), follow main path ↗ onto town wall embankment, keep going ↑

26.1 Just before "Speeltuin Kindervreugde" at footpath sign → (to Centrum & KP 30, LF 21b)

26.2 2nd rd ← (Van Linschotenstraat, to KP 30)

26.4 ⬳ 🛏 **Zuiderzeemuseum** (indoor section); for outdoor village buy tickets here; access at station

26.8 After Zuiderzeemuseum 1st rd → over bridge and immediately ↖ (to Station & KP 30, LF 21b)

26.9 1st rd ← (to Station & KP 30, LF 21b), dismount at bridge and walk through historic gate

27.1 Ep ↗ resume cycling on rd next to harbour (Drechterlandroute)

27.2 At end of rd ↖ (to Station) 🚗

27.4 ⬳ 🏠 🛈 🛏 🍽 ✈ **Enkhuizen** (station; end of route) Access Zuiderzeemuseum via ferry ("veerdienst")

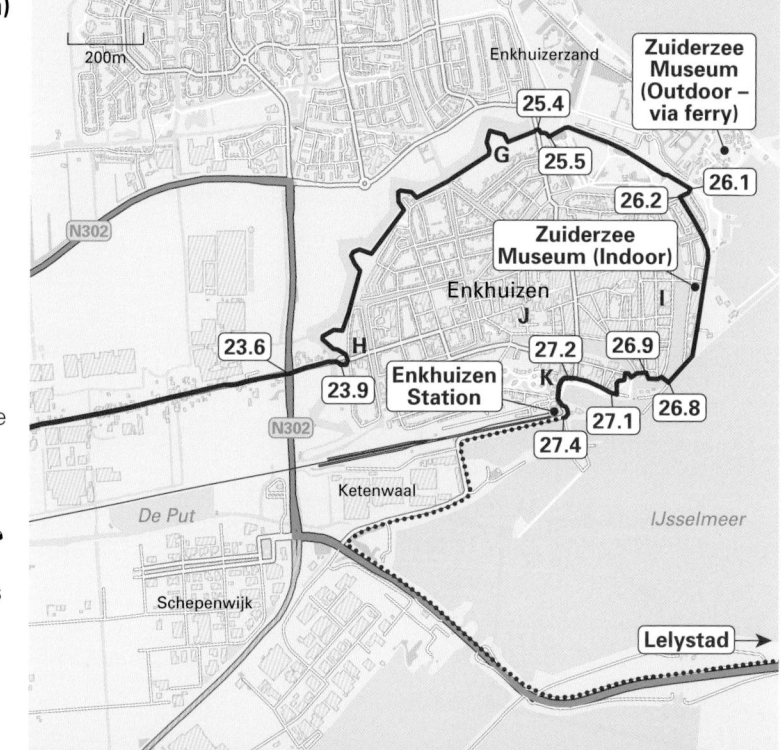

The track around "Markermeer" is only recommended for well-trained cyclists (see map and also page 12). Check the weather forecast before setting off and take plenty of food and drinks for the whole route you choose to do!

From Enkhuizen Station, follow route "Doorgaand Verkeer" and 🚲 signs to Lelystad. At the other end of the Enkhuizen-Lelystad Dam, you can either follow the 🚲 signs to Lelystad Centrum/Station to take the train to Amsterdam or continue cycling in Flevoland.

In that situation turn right at the end of the dam (🚲 route to Lelystad Haven). From here you can cycle to Almere via either the dead straight "Oostvaardersdijk", or move inland via the "Knardijk" and turn right via "Vogelweg". The dyke route offers great views over the Oostvaarders Plassen Nature Reserve with plenty of

bird-watching options. The inland route takes you through farmland, scattered with modern wind turbines.

When approaching Almere on both routes follow 🚲 signs to Amsterdam to get on the "Hollandse Brug" to the old mainland. Cycle via Muiderberg and Muiden to Weesp. Here you can either take the train to Amsterdam or join the main route to Maarssen/Utrecht at Amsterdam-Rijnkanaal (follow signs to Nigtevecht).

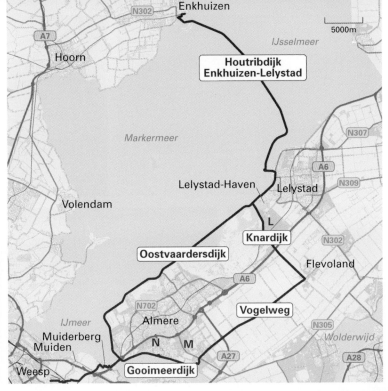

Section 18, 19, 20 (eastern): Maarssen – Nijmegen

The eastern route starts near Maarssen on a junction at the end of section 10 (main route Amsterdam-Maarssen). If you wish to start this route from a train station you'll need to travel to Breukelen. From there, use the short link route provided (see page 126). You can also use this link to return to the main route after completing the eastern route. In that case, you travel back from Nijmegen to Breukelen by train, followed by the link route to get to the start of section 11 (main route through Utrecht).

The eastern route takes you to an area which is clearly above sea level: The Utrecht Ridge ("Utrechtse Heuvelrug"). These sandy moorlands were pushed up during the last ice age and would actually form the Dutch coast if there were no Dutch people around to keep their lowlands dry. From Maarssen you'll gradually "climb" above sea level and you'll see the Dutch world slowly changing. First, you'll cycle on reclaimed land, but at the Tienhovense Plassen Nature Reserve you find yourself in an area of wetlands with forests on the horizon. These wetlands are fed by water descending from higher ground and the Dutch have never been able to reclaim this area fully. The area is great for bird-watching!

Cycle paths in Utrecht Ridge National Park and bird-watching in Tienhoven Nature Reserve.

At Hollandse Rading village you enter the forests of the Utrecht Ridge. Cycling in a peaceful, traffic-free setting on well-maintained paths is the biggest attraction here. Distances between places might feel long at times, but there are plenty of cool attractions hidden in the woods to keep everyone happy!

Lage Vuursche village almost entirely consists of pancake restaurants and attracts legions of walkers and cyclists. Lage Vuursche is also home to three 18-hole crazy golf courses, all part of the same park (Midgetgolf). Enter via the car park on arrival; open until 8 pm daily, prices vary.

The town of Soest is slightly off-route, but it provides some accommodation within easy reach (also a YHA). Soesterberg village is home to the Dutch military aviation museum ("Militaire Luchtvaart Museum") with a good collection of military planes (free entry, Mondays closed).

Deep in the woods you'll make your way to Austerlitz pyramid, erected by French troops in 1804 to celebrate French supremacy in continental Europe. From the top of the pyramid you have great views over the forest (admission € 3 pp, closed on Mondays, open daily in July/August). At the main car park near the pyramid you'll also find a fairground with restaurant ("Franse Tijd").

In Maarn, choose between more relaxed forest cycling or an alternative route via "Huis Doorn". The last German Kaiser (Wilhelm II) bought this estate in 1920 after fleeing his country during the 1918 revolution. He was buried in a mausoleum on the grounds after his death in 1941. The museum is open Tuesday-Sunday until 5 pm (admission € 9 pp).

The 1286 Amerongen Castle is an impressive fortified home, built on a strategic location next to the Nederrijn River and the high land travel corridor from Utrecht to the east. You can learn about its history via a visual display designed by British film director, Peter Greenaway.

From Amerongen you cross the Nederrijn River by ferry to be able to view the Utrecht Ridge from a distance. Cross back by the next ferry if you want to stay at YHA Elst. At Rhenen you return once more to the Utrecht Ridge to take in its remarkable Grebbeberg (see page 133). From there you take another ferry to Opheusden.

From here you'll cycle in the open landscape of the fruit-producing "Betuwe". In 1995, 250,000 people in this area were ordered to evacuate as extremely high water levels in the Rhine were likely to make the dykes burst. You'll cycle on the reinforced river dyke to Nijmegen with panoramic views over the shipping traffic on the Waal.

Section 18 (eastern): Maarssen – Soesterberg (27 km)

Link from Breukelen station (see map page 85):

0.0 At Breukelen station, go east via 🚲 (to Breukelen-Dorp)

0.1 At rndabt → via 🚲 on right-hand side onto bridge (to Breukelen-Dorp)

1.3 At rndabt ← via 🚲 crossings onto rd (to Loenen)

1.5 After car park immediately 1st rd → (Markt, later Dannestraat, to Scheendijk)

1.7 After bridge 1st rd → (Brugstraat)

1.8 After bridge → (to Maarssen/Utrecht & KP 46), continue on page 85 after 35.2 km

Start Eastern Route (see map on this page):

0.0 After 🛏 🍴 **Geesberge** (pub and terrace with river views) before bridge 1st rd ↙ (Machinekade), keep going ↑ (later Middenweg)

3.7 At T-jct ← (Laan van Niftarlake, to KP 49) 🚗

4.4 🛏 🍴 **Tienhoven** (café, after 100 m, ↑)

4.4 1st rd → (Dwarsdijk, to Hollandsche. Rading & KP 29)

5.2 At T-jct → via path with concrete strips (Kanaaldijk, to KP 29) into ↙ **Tienhovense Plassen Reserve**

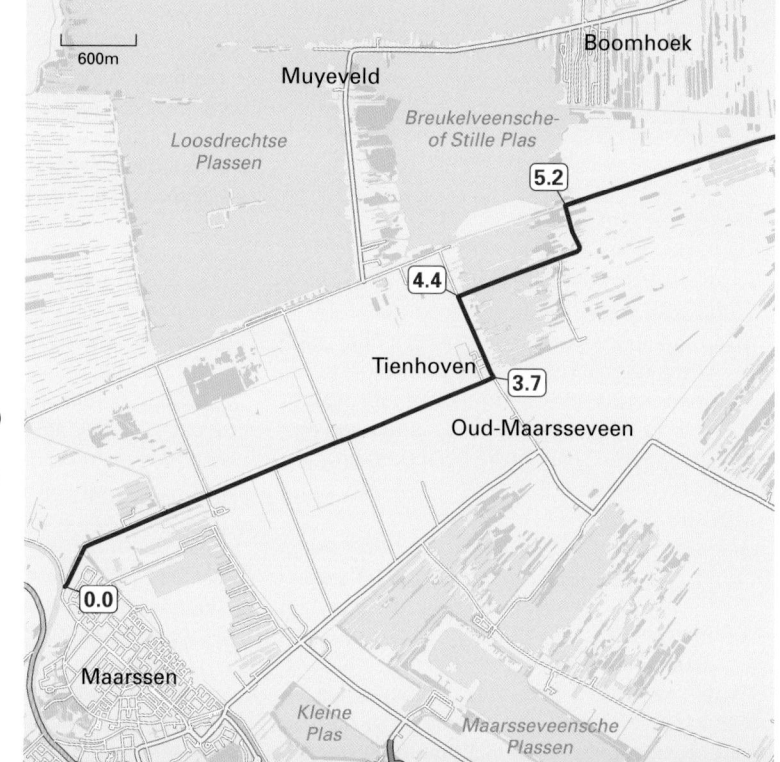

9.2 At KP 29 ↑ (Graaf Floris V weg, to Hollandsche Rading & KP 99)

11.5 At jct with lhts 🚗 ↑ (Vuurse Dreef, to Lage Vuursche & KP 82)

11.6 🚃 **Hollandsche Rading** (café at station)

11.6 ↑ via level crossing and motorway tunnel (Noorderparkroute)

11.9 At KP 82 ↑ (Vuurse Dreef, to KP 99)

Keep some space in your tummy for a pancake from the Dutch pancake capital, Lage Vuursche!

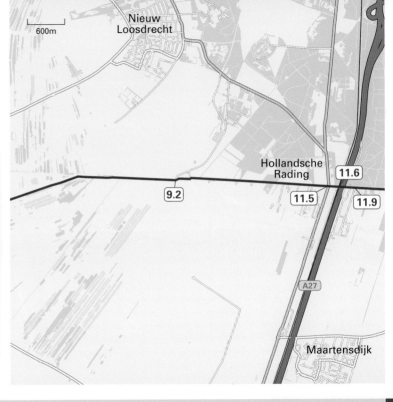

Section 18 (eastern): Maarssen – Soesterberg (27 km)

13.0 At T-jct of KP 99 ← (Vuurse Dreef, to Lage Vuursche & KP 63, LF 9b NAP route)

13.3 🚲 🍴 **De Paddestoel** (pancake restaurant)

13.4 At T-jct ← via "fietspad" on left-hand side of gravel rd (to Lage Vuursche & KP 63, LF 9b), keep following narrow 🚲 (moves later to right-hand side, Loosdrechts Spoor)

14.7 Ep ↑ via car park, at jct → (to Maartensdijk, LF 9b zuidelijke route) 🚗

14.9 🚂 🚲 🍴 **Lage Vuursche**

15.0 At end of village ↑ via "fietspad" on left-hand side (Vuursesteeg)

15.2 1st "fietspad" ← (to Soest, see "mushroom sign" 20562), narrow 🚲 on left-hand side of gravel rd

16.3 At sharp bend to the left at jct → via gravel rd into Landgoed Pijnenburg (Stulpselaan, to Soest), immediately ← via gravel rd (to Soest)

16.8 1st gravel rd → (Emilialaan, to Soest), follow bends to right and left

17.4 At sharp bend to the right ↑ via "fietspad"

17.6 Cross main rd 🚗🚗 ↑ via "fietspad" on right-hand side (Wieksloterweg WZ, to Soestduinen)

19.4 At KP 61 ↑ (to Soestduinen & KP 57)

19.8 At rd crossing ↑ via 🚲 (to Soest, Nieuwe Vuursche Route), later rd

20.5 🏘 **Soest** (1 km; ← via Bosstraat)

20.8 At KP 57 ↑ via level crossing and "fietspad" (to Soestduinen, Nieuwe Vuursche Route)

22.1 Ep → (to Den Dolder & KP 95), at KP 95 ← via level crossing, ↑ via rd (Paltzerweg)

24.0 At entrance of former NATO-base ↖ onto concrete rd (Verlengde Paltzerweg)

24.9 At T-jct of KP 55 → via 🚲 on right-hand side (Van Weerden Poelmanweg, to KP 52)

25.8 At T-jct with lhts → via 🚲 on right-hand side (Amersfoortse Straat, to Soesterberg & KP 52)

25.9 At next lhts ← via 🚲 crossing to KP 52 and immediately → via 🚲 on left-hand side (to Soesterberg, N237), keep going ↑ via 🚲

Happy cyclists in the Utrecht Ridge National Park.

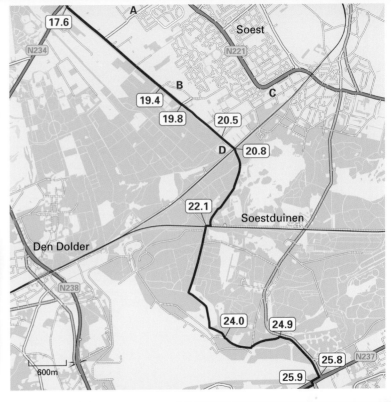

Section 19 (eastern): Soesterberg – Rhenen (35 km)

0.0 (27.1) In 🚉 🚌 🍴 **Soesterberg** at jct ← (Kampweg, to Austerlitz and ⛧ **Militaire Luchtvaart Museum**)

1.0 After bridge over motorway 1st rd → (Kampdwarsweg, to Austerlitz & KP 83)

1.4 At bend to the right ↑ via "fietspad" (to Austerlitz)

3.0 At KP 83 ↖ via "fietspad" (to Austerlitz & KP 1)

3.6 At KP 1 ↑ via "fietspad" (to Amersfoort)

4.0 At jct ↖ via "fietspad" (to Amersfoort)

5.5 At jct ← via "fietspad" (to Amersfoort)

5.7 At jct → via tarmac rd (to Amersfoort & KP 93) Caution: keep to the rd; military zone on left!

5.8 Note sign "ruiterpad" on right-hand side!

6.2 From "ruiterpad" sign, after a line of 50 trees on the right-hand side of rd → via footpath; walk bikes!

6.4 At T-jct of paths ← via horse-riding route and immediately → via footpath

6.6 At T-jct of paths ← and after 20 m → cut through bushes, then ↗ around pyramid

6.7 At entrance ⛧ **Pyramide van Austerlitz** → via main gravel path, resume cycling

7.1 Via ⛧ 🚌 🍴 **De Franse Tijd** cross main rd 🚗🚗, ← via 🚲 on right-hand side (to Woudenberg)

8.7 At jct with lhts ↑ via 🚲 crossing and → via 🚲 on left-hand side (to Maarn, N227), keep going ↑

The Austerlitz Pyramid.

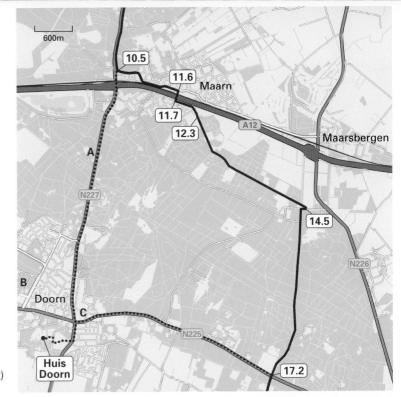

10.5 At jct of KP 6 ← (Poortse Bos, to Maarn & KP 89) 🚗

10.5 For a visit to ⮜ **Huis Doorn** ↑ via 🚲 along N227 to Doorn, to rejoin the main route follow 🚲 along N225 to Leersum, → at Darthuizen junction (after 17.2 km at top of next page)

11.6 🚻 🚲 **Maarn**
11.6 At jct "5 Mei Plein" → via rd tunnel (see also clock tower and sign "Heel de Heuvelrug Ronde 2")

11.7 After tunnel 1st rd ← (Kapelweg, later Buurtsteeg, to KP 7, Lustwaranderoute)

12.3 At end of rd ↑ via "fietspad" on left-hand side of gravel rd (to KP 7, later on right-hand side)

14.5 Ep (KP 7) ↘ via 🚲 on left-hand side and 1st rd ← (Wijkerweg, later Hoogstraat)

Section 19 (eastern): Soesterberg – Rhenen (35 km)

17.2 Cross main rd 🚗🚗
↑ (Darthuizerweg, to
Darthuizen)

19.1 At T-jct ← (Broekhuizerlaan,
to KP 11, LF 4a)

19.9 🌲 **Landgoed Broekhuizen**

19.9 At KP 11 ↑ (Middelweg, to
Leersum & KP 19, LF 4a
Rijndeltaroute)

20.5 In Leersum at jct 🡔
(Middelweg, ignore 🚲
routes)

21.2 At T-jct ← and at jct with lhts
→ via 🚲 on right-hand side
(Rijksstraatweg)

21.8 At rndabt ↑ via 🚲 on right-
hand side (Rijksstraatweg) via
shops 🍴 ☕ 🍽 ⚡ **Leersum**

23.4 In Amerongen at rndabt ↗ (to
Amerongen Castle & KP 17,
LF 4a Rijndeltaroute), at next
jct ↑ (Utrechtse Straatweg)

23.8 🍴 ☕ 🍽 ⚡ **Amerongen**

23.8 At jct with one-way streets
→ (Molenstraat)

24.0 At T-jct ← (opposite house
"Rodestein")

24.2 At T-jct →, at T-jct ← and
1st rd → (Rijnsteeg, to
Eck en Wiel)

24.2 🌲 **Amerongen Castle**
(150 m; see signs)

25.7 Via ferry across Nederrijn
River (charge ferry € 0.60
pp, cash only, runs daily
8 am-midnight)

26.0 At T-jct ← via short 🚲
on left-hand side, at next
jct ↑ via rd on dyke ridge
(Rijnbandijk, to Rhenen)

28.6 At KP 77 ↑ via dyke ridge rd (Rijnbandijk, to Rhenen,

28.6 🏠 🏕 ☕ 🍴 ⚓ **Elst** (1 km, via ferry; ← at KP 77)

31.1 At KP 9 1st rd ← (stay on dyke ridge rd, Marsdijk, to Rhenen & KP 92, later Rhenense Weg)

This dyke route offers splendid views over the town of Rhenen and the Grebbeberg further to the east. At the Grebbeberg the Utrecht Ridge comes abruptly to an end. It has played a critical role in Dutch military history. Controlled flooding has been the most important tool of defence for The Netherlands for centuries. In 1745 the "Grebbelinie" was created, a defensive line that would flood the land around the Utrecht Ridge, with military protecting the newly created shores. During the 1940 Nazi invasion the Dutch returned to this old line of defence. The Nazi approach over land was stopped by the Dutch army for three days at the Grebbeberg. Rhenen town ended up being in the line of fire and suffered severe damage. When the Germans finally pushed their way through, Rhenen's striking church tower was one of the few buildings still standing. On the Grebbeberg you'll pass various restaurants, a Dutch war cemetery and a zoo, "Ouwehand Dierenpark" (admission € 19 pp).

Section 20 (eastern): Rhenen – Nijmegen (31 km)

0.0 (= 35.2) Via footpath ↖ onto bridge across river, at end of footpath use 🚲 on left-hand side (N233)

0.7 After bridge immediately ↖ via 🚲 and immediately ↖ onto residential rd towards church tower (Trambaanweg)

1.0 After side rd "Duistere Weg" immediately ↗ via "fietspad", pass through barrier

1.3 Ep ↑ via rd, at rndabt → (Herenstraat) 🚗🚗

1.3 🏨 🚉 📷 🍴 ⚡ **Rhenen**

1.8 At 2 jcts with lhts ↑ via 🚲 on right-hand side (Grebbeweg, to Arnhem, N225)

2.6 🏨 📷 🍴 **Grebbeberg** (hotel & restaurants)

2.8 ⛲ **Ouwehand Dierenpark Zoo**

3.4 ⛲ **Militair Ereveld Grebbeberg** Caution: steep descent on main rd 🚗🚗

4.1 After descent at jct ↗ via dyke ridge rd (Grebbedijk, to Opheusden, LF 4a Rijndeltaroute)

5.1 1st rd → (to Opheusden)

6.0 Via ferry across Nederrijn River (charge ferry € 0.70 pp, cash only, daily until 8 pm, Sun 6 pm)

6.2 🏨 📷 🍴 **'t Veerhuis ("Fietsstop")** at ferry landing

6.5 At jct of KP 94 ↖ via dyke ridge rd (Rijnbandijk, to Centrum & KP 19) 🚗

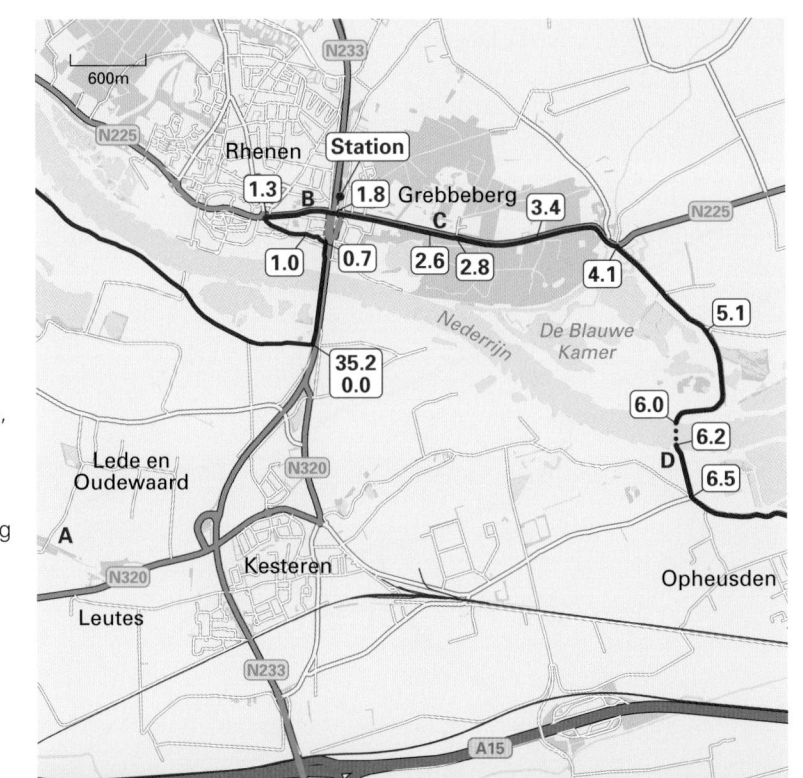

7.3 At KP 19 follow main rd → down into village (to Centrum & KP 18) 🚗

7.5 🚉 **Opheusden**

7.6 After shops at jct ← (Lodderstraat, to KP 18 & Dodewaard, later Dalwagenseweg) 🚗

8.8 Just before level crossing and station ← (Dalwagen, to KP 18)

10.3 1st rd ← (De Zandvoort, to Hemmen & KP 18, later Boelehamsestraat)

11.3 At KP 18 follow rd → via level crossing (Kerkstraat, to Dodewaard), keep going ↑

13.1 At T-jct of KP 16 ← via dyke ridge rd (Waalbandijk, to Nijmegen & KP 17)

13.6 📷 🍴 **"De Engel"** (pub/café)

13.6 At jct of KP 17 ↗ via dyke ridge rd (Waalbandijk, to Nijmegen & KP 58), keep going ↑

Crossing the Nederrijn River by ferry.

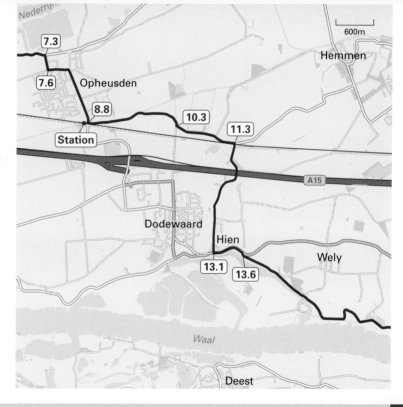

Section 20 (eastern): Rhenen – Nijmegen (31 km)

19.0 At jct before motorway
bridge over river ↑
(to Nijmegen & KP 17),
keep going ↑

21.8 🛒 **Farm Shop
"Landwinkel"**

22.7 ⛲ ⛱ **Slijk Ewijk**
(church with picnic table)

*Have a break overlooking the Rhine arm Waal. On arrival in The Netherlands,
the Rhine River splits into three arms: the IJssel to the north and the Nederrijn
and Waal to the west. The Waal is the widest arm, taking most of the Rhine's
water flow. Ending in Rotterdam it is also one of the busiest inland shipping
routes of the world.*

24.5 📍 🍴 **"De Altena"** (pub/café)

29.2 On arrival in Lent after tunnel under railway ➤ (Snelbinder, to KP 19), dismount and walk bike up steps, then ← via 🚲 bridge to other side of river

The "Snelbinder" cycle bridge takes you into the heart of Nijmegen.

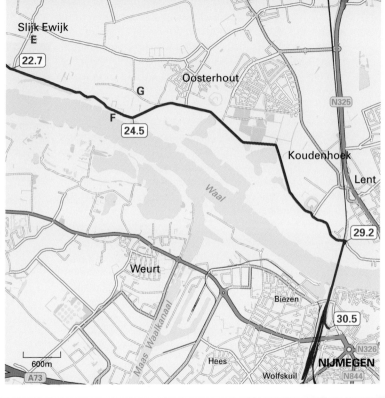

Section 21 (eastern): Nijmegen and beyond (24 km)

The Nijmegen Bridge, scene of the Allied advance during Operation Market Garden in WWII. The famous war film "A Bridge Too Far" was partly shot here. The bridge is also in the centre of the action during the Nijmegen walking event, "Vierdaagse".

Nijmegen was founded by the Romans and recently celebrated 2,000 years of existence. Most traces of its Roman past have vanished, but in the Valkhof Museum you'll find various Roman artifacts on display, alongside plenty of modern art (Mondays closed, admission € 7 pp). Another museum "must" in Nijmegen is the Dutch Cycling Museum Velorama, with a collection of 250 historic bicycles, including the 1817 "hobby horse". It is located on the quay (open daily, admission € 5 pp).

Nijmegen is a bustling university town and the third week of July is Nijmegen's highlight of the year. During this week the famous Nijmegen four-day walk, "Vierdaagse", is held, attracting up to 40,000 walkers from around the world. The walk is extremely popular with war veterans, as Nijmegen was a focal point in the Allied liberation of The Netherlands during WWII.

Away from the city you'll find the National Liberation Museum. Plan a full day for a visit. The 1944 and 1945 artifacts and excellent displays about Operation Market Garden won't leave you disappointed. Note: the circular route from Nijmegen is a slightly demanding ride with some serious steep climbs to take in; allow plenty of time!

0.0 (= 30.5) End of 🚲 bridge route
- For Nijmegen station →
- For city centre and circular route via National Liberation Museum see below:

0.0 At end of 🚲 bridge route ← via right-hand side of rd (to Weurt & KP 20, LF 3b Maasroute) 🚗

0.2 At T-jct ← via 🚲 at right-hand side of rd (to Weurt & KP 20, LF 3b Maasroute)

0.4 🚶 🏠 🚉 🛒 🍴 ⚡ **Nijmegen** (For city centre → at T-jct)

0.4 At T-jct ← via 🚲 at right-hand side of rd (to Weurt & KP 20, LF 3b Maasroute), then 1st rd → via 🚲 at right-hand side of rd (to Waalkade, LF 3b Maasroute), later join rd 🚗

1.2 At rndabt ↑ via quay rd (LF 3b Maasroute) 🚗

1.7 At jct before historic river bridge ↖ (Ubbergseweg, to "Doorgaand Verkeer", LF 3b Maasroute), pass under historic river bridge 🚗, keep going ↑

Operation Market Garden intended to bypass German defence lines by an ambitious northern advance. The aim, Arnhem (north of Nijmegen), turned out to be "a bridge too far", but the Nijmegen Bridge was taken by Allied forces successfully. German attempts to blow up the bridge were sabotaged, probably by Dutch Resistance hero, Jan van Hoof.

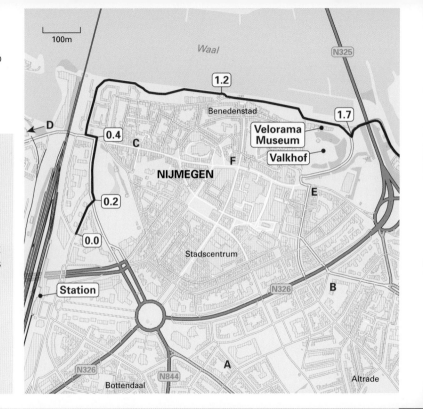

Section 21 (eastern): Nijmegen and beyond

Read on right for continued route to Liberation Museum →

Liberation Museum to Nijmegen:

6.4 Ep at KP 9 cross rd 🚗🚗, ← via 🚲 at right-hand side (to Malden & KP 10, LF 3b)

7.2 After level crossing at KP 10 2nd rd → (Heyendaalseweg)

7.9 At KP 6 cross jct ↑ 🚗🚗 onto 🚲 at right-hand side (to Universiteit & KP 5)

8.3 At rndabt ↑ (to Centrum)

8.9 At jct with lhts ↑ via 1st 🚲 crossing, then ← via next 🚲 crossing and → via 🚲 at left-hand side (to KP 5)

9.0 1st rd ← at KP 5 (to KP 17)

9.6 At rd crossing with lhts ↑ (to KP 17 & Nijmegen CS)

9.9 At KP 17 → via 🚲 on bridge

10.0 After bridge ← via lhts onto 🚲 (to Nijmegen CS)

11.2 Ep ↖ to station, end of route

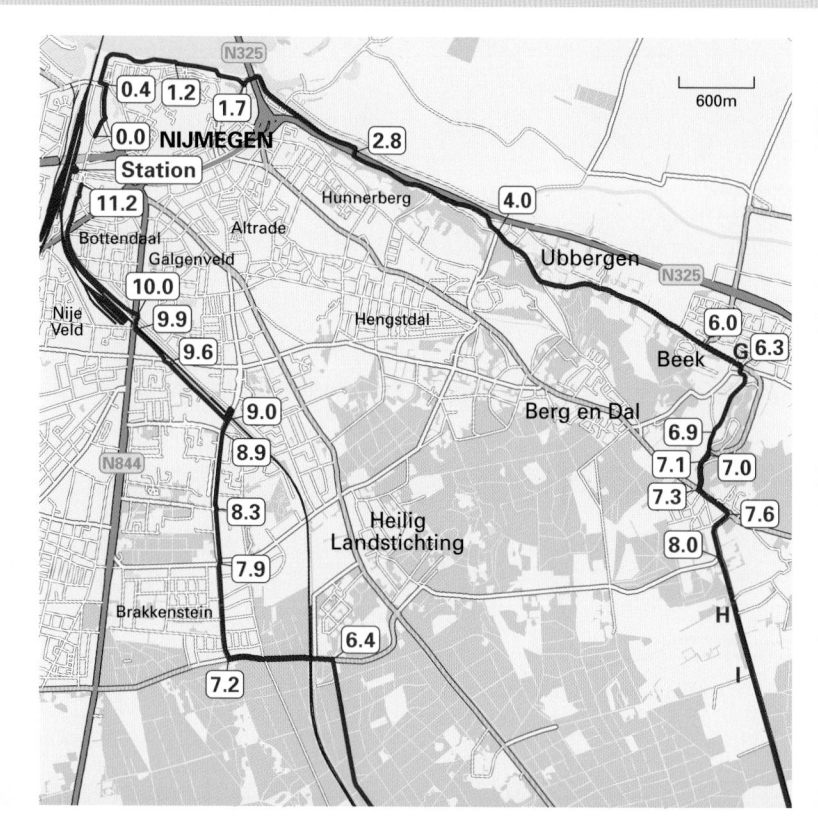

Nijmegen to Liberation Museum:

2.8 Cross main rd 🚗🚗 and ← via paved rd (Ubbergseweg)

4.0 Follow "Rijksstraatweg" ↗ (paved rd, to KP 62)

6.0 At jct of KP 62 ↑ via paved rd (to Berg en Dal & KP 61)

6.3 🏠 🛏 🍴 **Beek** (hotels)

6.3 1st rd → (Nieuwe Holleweg), then 1st rd ← via steep climb (Van der Veurweg/Bosweg)

6.9 At rndabt ↖ via paved rd

7.0 At T-jct dismount, cross rd and → via footpath on right-hand side (Nieuwe Holleweg)

7.1 Ep ↗ via rd, at end ↖ 🚗

7.3 At T-jct ← (Kleefse Baan, to Groesbeek & KP 59) 🚗🚗

7.4 🏠 🛏 🍴 **Berg en Dal** (hotels)

7.6 At rndabt → via 🚲 at right-hand side (to Groesbeek)

8.0 At jct where 🚲 bends to right (KP 59) ← cross rd and ↑ via 🚲 on right-hand side (to KP 29)

Read on right for route to Liberation Museum →

Liberation Museum to Nijmegen:

0.0 (13.1) At end of driveway Liberation Museum ← via 🚲 on left-hand side of rd (to Groesbeek)

0.1 ⛺ 📷 🍴 **De Oude Molen**

0.1 At T-jct → via 🚲 on right-hand side of rd (Nieuweweg, to Nijmegen)

0.3 At KP 28 ↑ via 🚲 on right-hand side of rd (to KP 31)

1.4 At bend to right (begin "Nijmeegsebaan") at KP 31 ← cross rd 🚗🚗, then ↗ (Maldensebaan, to Malden & KP 32), join "fietspad" on left-hand side of gravel rd

3.5 At T-jct of KP 32 → via 🚲 on left-hand side of gravel rd (to Nijmegen & KP 9), keep going ↑ Continue reading on left-hand side of page above!

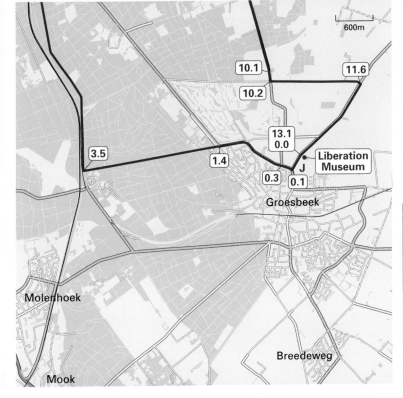

Nijmegen to Liberation Museum:

10.1 ⮜ **Canadian War Cemetery**

10.2 At KP 29 ← cross rd 🚗 (Derde Baan, to KP 84)

11.6 At T-jct of KP 84 → via 🚲 on left-hand side of rd (Wylerbaan, to KP 28)

13.1 ⮜ **Liberation Museum** "Nationaal Bevrijdingsmuseum 1944-1945", end of route; read on left side of this page for return journey to Nijmegen

Section 22 (southern): Vlissingen – Breezand (34 km)

You'll follow the coast of the former island of Walcheren, starting in nautical Vlissingen on the Westerschelde estuary. This is the only estuary in the southwest of The Netherlands that wasn't dammed after the 1953 floods, as it is the shipping route to the Antwerp docks in Belgium. On the promenade, the Michiel de Ruyter statue looks proudly over the waves. This is Flushing's famous admiral, responsible for England's biggest naval defeat: the 1667 raid on the Medway. The Dutch captured the town of Sheerness, burnt three main ships at the Chatham naval base and towed away the flagship of the English fleet. The spirit of piracy is kept high in the former armoury "Het Arsenaal", a pirate theme park with sea aquarium and viewing tower (open daily, admission € 14 pp). The "Muzeeum" displays Zeeland's past more seriously (open daily, admission € 8 pp).

The Walcheren coast consists of a narrow strip of sand dunes with small seaside resorts like Zoutelande and Domburg. There are countless access points to Walcheren's sandy beach, only to be interrupted by an impressive tarmac sea wall at Westkapelle. It was bombed in 1944 by allied forces to literally drown the Nazi defences, causing flooding of the whole island.

The Westerschelde estuary.

0.0	From main entrance Vlissingen Station walk ↑ via walkway with zebra-pattern (to Centrum, LF 1b)
0.1	Walk through lock area ↖ onto 🚲, start cycling
0.4	At end lock area ↖ via 🚲 (to Arsenaal, LF 1b), follow route onto sea barrier boulevard
2.0	◁ **Het Arsenaal**
2.0	Dismount and walk through lock area
2.1	◁ 🏠 🚾 📷 🍴 ⚕ **Vlissingen**
2.1	Ep ← via rd (to Boulevard & KP 81) 🚗, becomes one-way rd with contra flow for cyclists
2.2	◁ **Promenade (statue Michiel de Ruyter)**
3.0	At jct ↑ via rd with contra flow for cyclists (Boulevard Bankert, to Koudekerke) 🚗

Vlissingen Harbour is home to various pilot boats, needed to bring big container ships safely through the treacherous Westerschelde estuary to the Antwerp docks in Belgium.

Section 22 (southern): Vlissingen – Breezand (34 km)

4.1 At T-jct ← via 🚲 on left-hand side (Kenau Hasselaarstraat, to Koudekerke)

4.1 ⚓ **Vlissingen Nollestrand**

4.2 1st rd ← (Nollehoofd) and immediately ↗ via "fietspad" on sand dune ridge (to KP 81)

5.7 After descent at jct ↑ via "fietspad" on left-hand side (to KP 81)

6.7 At jct opposite "Golden Tulip Hotel" ↟ via rd 🚐 (to Zoutelande & KP 80)

7.6 1st "fietspad" ↖ (to Zoutelande & KP 80)

8.1 🏠 🍴 🍽 ⚓ 🔧 **Dishoek**

8.1 Ep on square → via 🚲 on right-hand side (to Zoutelande & KP 80)

8.2 At jct ← via "fietspad" (to Zoutelande & KP 80), at KP 80 ↑ via tarmac "fietspad" (to KP 44),

10.5 🍴 🍽 ⚓ **Valkenisse** (restaurant on cycle route)

10.8 At KP 44 ↑ via "fietspad" (to Zoutelande & KP 42)

11.3 Ep ↑ via paved rd (Duinweg)

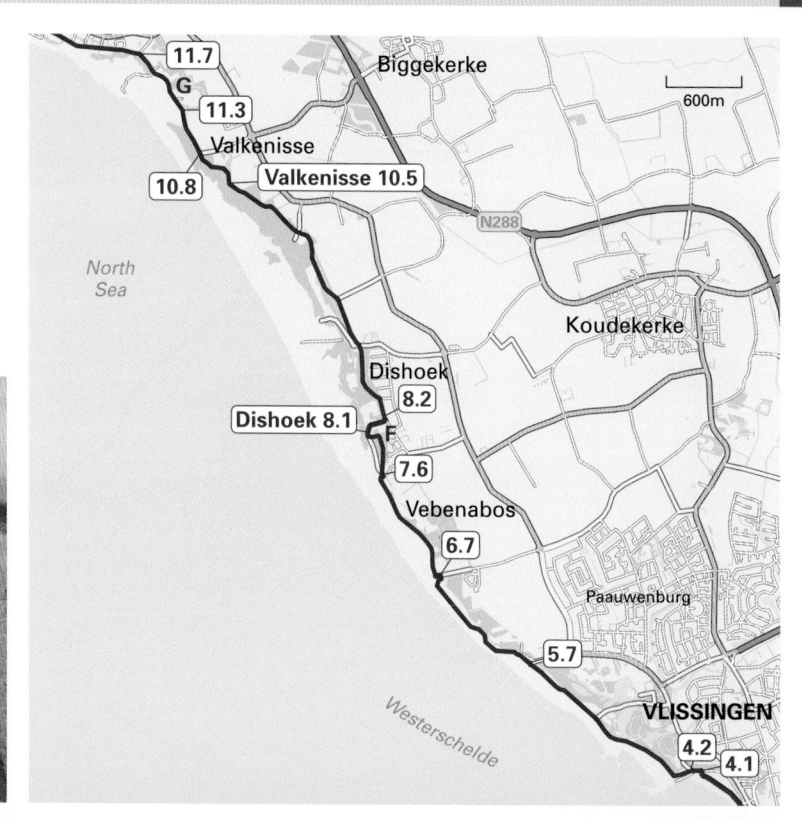

11.7 At jct ↑ (Duinweg), one-way rd with contra flow for cyclists, keep going ↑ (to KP 42) 🚗

12.5 🏠 🚉 📷 🍴 ⚓ ⚡ **Zoutelande**

12.5 At jct ↑ (Langstraat, to Westkapelle) 🚗

12.9 After church at jct ↖ via 🚲 on right-hand side, after 50 m cross rd 🚗 ↑ to 🚲 on left-hand side (to Westkapelle)

13.6 After sign leaving Zoutelande 1st "fietspad" ↖ (to Westkapelle & KP 10)

15.9 ⚓ **Scheldezicht** (beach access only)

15.9 Ep ↗ via tarmac rd and immediately ↖, after 50 m → via "fietspad" (to KP 10)

16.1 At jct ↖ via 🚲 through forest (to KP 10)

17.0 Ep ↑ via rd, at T-jct ← via 🚲 on left-hand side (D'Arke, to Domburg & KP 10)

17.3 🚉 📷 🍴 ⚓ ⚡ **Westkapelle** (for shops → via rd)

17.3 ↑ via 🚲 (to Domburg & KP 10), keep going ↑

17.5 ⚞ **Liberty Bridge** (bridge to tank on dyke ridge)

18.5 ⚞ 📷 🍴 **De Westkaap** (on Westkapelle sea wall)

19.0 At lighthouse 1st rd ← stay on seawall rd (Noorderhoofdweg, to KP 10)

Section 22 (southern): Vlissingen – Breezand (34 km)

20.9 At end of seawall rd at KP 10 ← via 🚲 on left-hand side (to KP 14)

21.9 1st rd → (Trommelweg)

22.4 1st rd ↖ (Babelweg)

23.4 At T-jct → (Kromme Weg)

23.8 1st rd ← (Schansweg, later Prinsenpark)

24.5 At T-jct ← (Brouwerijweg, keep going ↑) Caution: give way to traffic from the right!

25.1 At T-jct → via 🚲 on right-hand side

25.2 2nd rd ← via one-way street with contra flow for cyclists (Zuidstraat, to Oostkapelle)

25.4 At T-jct → via one-way street with contra flow for cyclists (to Oostkapelle) 🚗

25.5 🏠 🛆 📷 🍴 ⚓ ⚓ **Domburg** (for beach ← via rd)

25.5 At jct ↑ via 🚲 on right-hand side (Domburgseweg, to Oostkapelle & KP 16)

25.9 At jct ↖ via 🚲 on right-hand side (Domburgseweg, to Oostkapelle & KP 16)

26.8 At house "Wijde Landen" cross rd 🚗 ↑ to 🚲 on left-hand side (to Vrouwenpolder & KP 16)

27.0 1st rd ← (Duinvlietweg, to Vrouwenpolder)

27.4 At barrier → via gravel "fietspad" (to Vrouwenpolder & KP 16), keep going ↑

28.8 At KP 16 ↑ via "fietspad"
(to Vrouwenpolder & KP 27),
keep going ↑ via gravel &⃝

28.9 ⌇ **Lage duintjes**
(beach access only)

29.6 🅿 ⍩ ⌇ **Oostkapelle**
(for beach ← via rd)

29.6 Cross rd 🚗 ↑ via "fietspad"
(to Vrouwenpolder)

30.3 Ep ↖ via rd (to
Vrouwenpolder & KP 27),

later paved rd (Kon.
Emmaweg)

32.0 At T-jct of KP 27 ↖ via &⃝
on left-hand side (to Burgh-
Haamstede)

32.2 1st rd ← (to Burgh-
Haamstede & KP 30)

32.3 ⛺ 🅿 ⍩ **Oranjezon**

32.3 1st "fietspad" → (to Burgh-
Haamstede & KP 30), keep
going ↑, later via rd

Domburg.

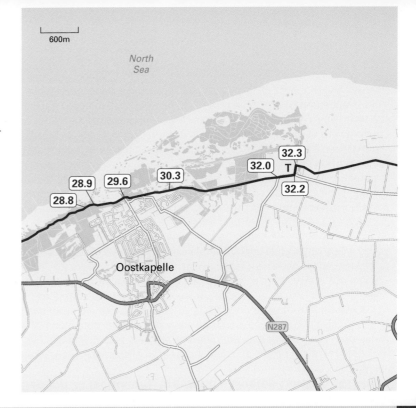

Section 23 (southern): Breezand – Goeree Landing (43 km)

From the holiday village of Breezand you ride across the big Delta Plan dams. You start with the shortest, the Veerse Gat Dam. This dam was completed in 1961 and since then new beaches and sand dunes have formed in front of the dam. Just 2 kilometres further on you'll arrive at the massive Oosterschelde barrier (see below). Have a break halfway at the visitor centre, Deltapark Neeltje Jans, where you'll find excellent exhibitions about the 1953 floods, the construction works and Oosterschelde National Park. An estuary cruise and visit to a seal centre is also included (open daily, admission € 15 pp).

On arrival on the former island of Schouwen you first cycle by the small harbour of Burghsluis, where you can join more estuary cruises. Then you cycle via the mysterious and lonely church tower of the drowned village of Koudekerke before making your way to Burgh-Haamstede. This is the main town of the island, mostly catering for holidaymakers staying at nearby campsites and holiday parks. Schouwen's sand dune reserves are extensive and a joy to explore by bike. The route takes you via one of the widest and emptiest beaches of The Netherlands, the "Verklikkerstrand", before taking on the Brouwersdam to the former island of Goeree.

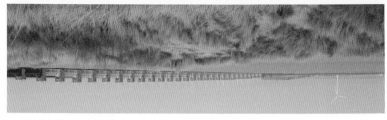

0.0 (= 34.0) At T-jct ← via one-way rd with cyclists contra flow (Vroondijk, to Burgh-Haamstede & KP 30)

1.3 🅿 🍴 ⚓ **Breezand** (via footpath)

1.5 On bend to right at 🏨 🅿 🍴 **Duinoord** (hotel) ← via rd closed for motorised traffic, pass barrier (to Burgh-Haamstede & KP 3)

2.0 ⚞ **Delta Plan: Veerse Gat Dam**

4.5 At KP 3 ↑ (to KP 4, LF 1b Noordzeeroute), at end of dam ↗ via narrow "fietspad", keep going ↑

6.1 At KP 4 ← (to KP 70, LF 1b Noordzeeroute)

6.3 ⚞ **Delta Plan: Oosterschelde barrier (Roompot)** This barrier was constructed over a period of eight years and cost € 2.5 billion, heavily exceeding its budget. In 1984, two years before completion, the Dutch government decided to build one floodgate less to save some money. The pillar for this floodgate was already built and still stands lonely in the docks near the visitor centre. The reclaimed island Neeltje Jans functioned as a building site and was connected to the mainland by a temporary two-mile bridge. The barrier has 62 floodgates; pillars are 30 to 40 metres high. A floodgate spans 42 metres and the metal doors weigh 480 tons each. Silt is causing corrosion to the mechanism and doors, leaving the Dutch with an annual maintenance bill of at least € 10 million.

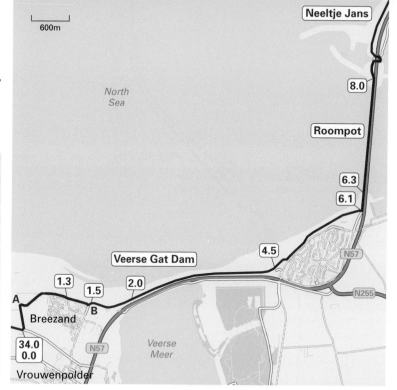

Section 23 (southern): Breezand – Goeree Landing (43 km)

8.0 ⟨ **Delta Plan:
Neeltje Jans island**

8.3 🛏 🍴 **De Helling** (snackbar)

8.4 Cross lock area, then
immediately ↖ (LF 1b), keep
going ↑ via wide tarmac dam

11.1 ⟨ 🛏 **Delta Plan: Delta Park
Neeltje Jans** (for exhibition
centre → at jct, follow

🚲 route)

11.1 At jct ↑ (Hoogh-Plaetweg,
to KP 70, LF 1b)

11.9 ⟨ **Delta Plan: Oosterschelde
barrier (Schaar)**

12.9 ⟨ **Delta Plan:
Roggeplaat island**

13.5 ⟨ **Delta Plan: Oosterschelde
barrier (Hammen)**

*Across the Oosterschelde barrier you'll cycle past the lonely Koudekerke
church tower. According to local legend, the village drowned hundreds of years
ago because fishermen captured a mermaid, the wife of a King Neptune-type
character. He begged the fishermen to give his wife back, but they just laughed.
Then he spoke his fatal words, "I will let your village drown and only the tower
will survive!"*

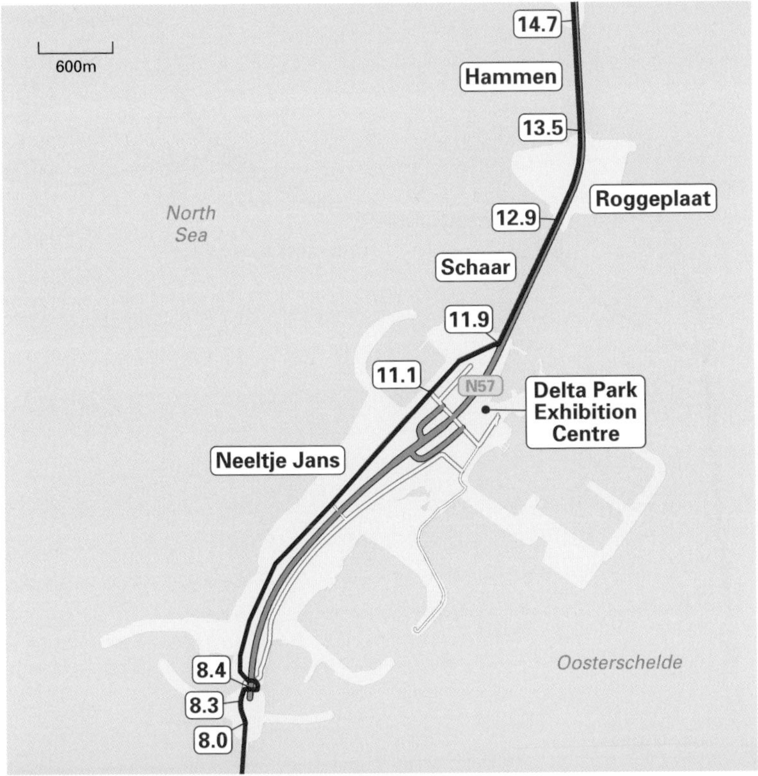

600m

North
Sea

14.7

Hammen

13.5

Roggeplaat

12.9

Schaar

11.9

11.1

N57

Neeltje Jans

Delta Park
Exhibition
Centre

8.4

8.3

8.0

Oosterschelde

14.7 At end of barrier at KP 70 ↑ (to KP 71)

15.3 At jct → via tunnel (Westerseweg, to KP 71)

16.0 At T-jct → (to KP 71, Strijd tegen water route)

16.1 1st rd → and after 50 m ↙ via gravel "fietspad" (to KP 71, leads to tarmac sea wall)

17.8 Ep before lighthouse ← via tarmac rd (to KP 71)

17.8 👀 🍽 **Burghsluis** (harbour and café)

18.0 At T-jct → via rd on dyke ridge (Havenweg)

18.1 🚣 **Oosterschelde National Park estuary cruises** (Landing "Rederij Roermond"; various tours)

18.5 At end of rd ↗ (Plompetorenweg)

19.7 🚣 **Plompe Toren (drowned village Koudekerke)** Fun, free exhibition in the tower (open daily)

19.7 After tower 1st rd ← (Koudekerkseweg)

20.6 At jct ← (Brabersweg)

21.4 At jct →

22.6 Cross rd 🚗🚗 ↑ (Zandweg)

22.9 On bend to left ↗ (Zandweg), keep going ↑ via one-way streets (Ooststraat, later Ring)

23.4 🏠 🏪 👀 🍽 🍴 **Burgh-Haamstede**

23.4 At T-jct ←, follow bend ↗ 🚗 (Weststraat, to Westenschouwen, KP 73, LF 1a Noordzeeroute)

24.0 👀 🍽 **De Pannenkoekenmolen** (pancake restaurant in windmill)

24.0 At KP 73 1st rd ↘ (Moolweg, to KP 76)

24.8 At jct ↖ (Vertonsweg, to KP 76)

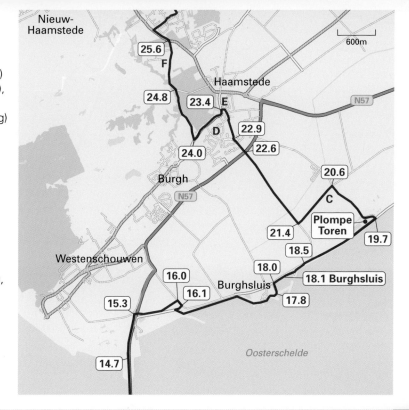

Section 23 (southern): Breezand – Goeree Landing (43 km)

25.6 At T-jct ← via 🚲 on right-hand side (Kloosterweg)

25.8 At jct 1st rd → (Westerenbanweg)

26.0 At jct "Binnendwarsweg" ↑

26.3 1st rd ← (closed for motorised traffic)

26.7 At barrier ↑ (Maireweg)

26.7 🍴 **'t Lapje** (crazy golf & café)

27.2 At sharp bend to the left ↑ via "fietspad" (Duinhoevepad, to Strand)

28.5 🔭 🌲 **Viewpoint Verklikkersstrand**

28.7 ⚓ **Verklikkersstrand** (beach access only)

28.7 At start beach → via gravel 🚲

30.2 Ep → via concrete path

30.5 After bike park ← via gravel "fietspad" (to KP 76)

31.3 At ⚓ **Wilhelminahoeve** ↑ via "fietspad" (to KP 76)

32.4 At ⚓ **Jan van Renesseweg** ↗ through bike park and ↖ onto rd (Duinweg, to KP 76)

33.0 At KP 76 ↑ via gravel "fietspad" (to KP 84)

33.7 🏠 🍴 **Zeerust**

33.7 Ep ↖ onto rd (Rampweg, to KP 84) 🚗

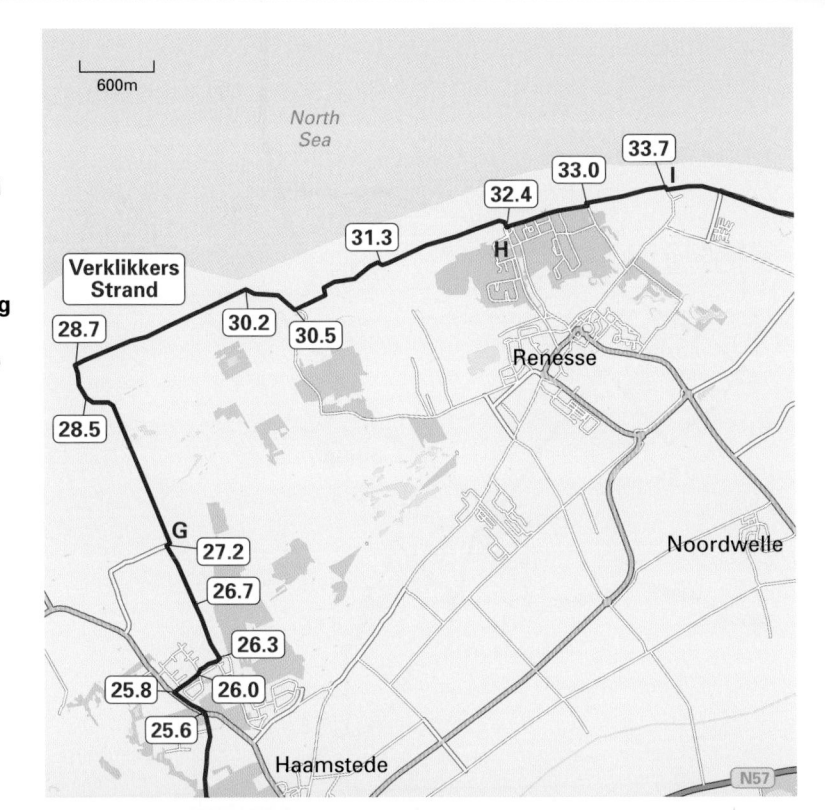

35.6 1st "fietspad" ↑ tarmac rd on dyke ridge

35.9 At ⟍ **Ellemeet** ↑ onto ♠

36.4 ♠ ⊮ **De Wijde Wereld** (snackbar, circle car park)

36.4 At jct ← via ♠ on left-hand side (to Rotterdam)

36.7 Cross rd ↑ via ♠ on right-hand side on dam ridge

36.7 ⟨ **Delta Plan: Brouwersdam**

39.7 ⟍ ♠ ⊮ **Brouwersdam** (beach pavilion; ← at jct)

39.7 At jct ↑ via ♠ on dam ridge (to Ouddorp & KP 51)

Cycle path on the ridge of the Brouwersdam.

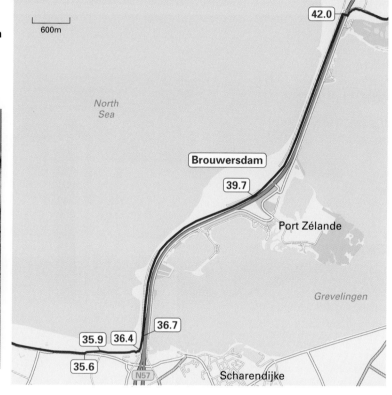

North Sea

600m

42.0

Brouwersdam

39.7

Port Zélande

Grevelingen

36.7

35.9 36.4

35.6

N57

Scharendijke

Section 24 (southern): Goeree Landing – Europoort (42 km)

From your "landing" at the former island of Goeree, you ride along Lake Grevelingen to the inland town of Ouddorp, which mostly caters for holidaymakers. From here, the route takes you to the small, scenic town of Goedereede. This town (literally meaning "safe anchorage") received city rights in 1312 and had a thriving trading and fishing port, but sedimentation slowly closed the port off from the sea, ending the town's wealth.

The Haringvlietdam is the main outlet for both the Rhine and Maas Rivers, and consists of 17 sluices. A European environmental campaign hopes to see the sluice gates permanently opened (like in the Oosterschelde barrier), so tides can return to the Haringvliet estuary.

Voorne is the last former island on your journey and here you cycle across flat and open farmland to Brielle. This scenic town is encircled by fine fortifications, reflecting its fight against Spanish rule during the Dutch war of independence. Stroll through Dutch history in the local Brielle museum on the market square (admission € 2 pp) and stay overnight in Brielle as needed, as this is the last place where you can stay before cycling into the vast Rotterdam Europoort (see also pages 40 and 41).

(Top) Cycling along Lake Grevelingen to Goedereede (Below).

0.0 (42.8) Ep ("Goeree Landing") at T-jct of KP 51 → via 🚲 tunnel (to Grevelingen & KP 52)

0.1 After tunnel ← (to Ouddorp & KP 52), route becomes 🚲 on right-hand side, keep going ↑

1.8 Ep → via rd (to Ouddorp & KP 52)

3.1 At jct of KP 52 ↑ (to KP 58), rd becomes path

5.4 🍴 🍽 **Ouddorp Haven** (harbour & café, at jct →)

5.4 At jct ↑ via path on dyke ridge (to KP 58)

5.6 Ep ↗ via rd (to KP 58)

5.7 At jct 58 ← via bridge, after bridge → (to Ouddorp & KP 57)

5.9 1st gravel path ↖ to wooden footbridge, then ↑ via 🚲 (to Centrum & KP 57)

6.3 1st rd → (to KP 57)

6.5 1st 🚲 ← (into Ouddorp, to KP 57)

6.8 Ep → and at T-jct ← via 🚲 crossing (to Ouddorp & KP 57) 🚗

7.2 🏠 🍴 🍴 🍽 🍴 **Ouddorp** (town centre ← at jct)

7.2 At jct of KP 57 ↑ (to KP 56) 🚗

7.6 At rndabt ↗ (Hofdijksweg, to Goedereede) 🚗

7.8 At rndabt ↑ via 🚲 crossing (to Goedereede)

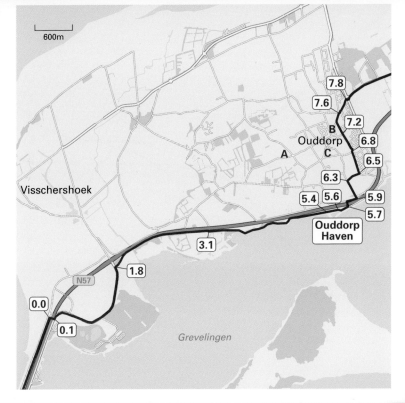

600m

Visschershoek

Ouddorp

A B C

Grevelingen

N57

Ouddorp Haven

Section 24 (southern): Goeree Landing – Europoort (42 km)

9.6 2nd rd → via dyke ridge rd (Middeldijk, to KP 61)

10.6 1st 🚲 ← (Spuidijk, to KP 61, LF 1b)

11.4 In Goedereede 1st rd → (Pieterstraat, to KP 61)

11.5 ⬅🏠🛆🍴 **Goedereede**

11.5 At town square ↑ (Markt, LF 1b Noordzeeroute)

11.7 At jct ↗ via tarmac 🚲

(Kinderdijk, LF 1b)

11.9 At rd crossing ↑ via 🚲 (to Havenhoofd, KP 62, LF 1b Noordzeeroute)

14.0 Ep ↑ via rd (Haveneind, to Brielle, LF 1b)

14.5 At end of Havenhoofd village ↗ via 🚲 on left-hand side (Meester Snijderweg, to KP 64)

Picturesque Goedereede.

16.7 After tunnel under main rd, at rndabt ← via 🚲 on right-hand side (to Brielle, LF 1b Noordzeeroute), join rd before bridge 🚗

17.2 After bridge at jct ↑ via rd closed for motorised traffic (to Brielle & KP 21, LF 1b Noordzeeroute)

17.5   🚲 🍽 **Delta Plan: Haringvliet Expo** (exhibition in restaurant overlooking Haringvliet)

17.7   **Delta Plan: Haringvlietdam**

21.4 1st rd ← (Onderlangs, to Brielle)

22.0 After tunnel at T-jct ← (Krommeweg, to Brielle)

Haringvlietdam.

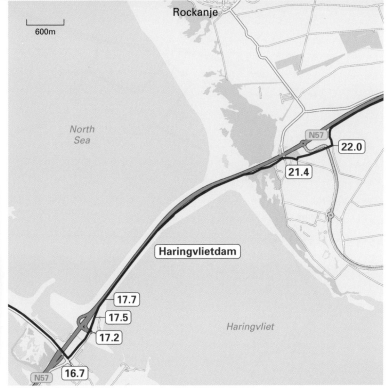

Section 24 (southern): Goeree Landing – Europoort (42 km)

23.5 1st 🚲 ← (to Brielle)

24.2 After rd crossing 🚗 at 🚲 T-jct ← via 🚲 tunnel, after tunnel ↑ via 🚲 on right-hand side

24.8 1st rd → (Bredeweg, later Goolseweg)

26.2 1st rd ← (Sliklandseweg)

26.8 1st rd ← (Middenweg)

27.6 1st rd → (Sluisweg)

29.2 At T-jct cross rd 🚗 ↑, then ← via 🚲 on right-hand side (to KP 32)

29.9 1st rd ↗ (Oude Dijk)

30.0 ☞ **De Vuijle Vaatdoek** (Art gallery & café)

30.2 In bend to the right ↖ (Oude Dijk)

30.4 ↑ via car park onto "fietspad" (to KP 31)

31.8 At T-jct ← via 🚲 on right-hand side (to KP 31)

32.3 After bridge immediately → via 🚲 (to KP 31), at next jct keep ↗ via path along canal

32.6 At T-jct → via 🚲 on right-hand side, after bridge immediately ← cross rd 🚗🚗 onto 🚲 (Kaaisingel)

33.1 Ep ← via 🚲 on right-hand side (Oostdam), join rd at town gate ↑ 🚗 (Kaaistraat)

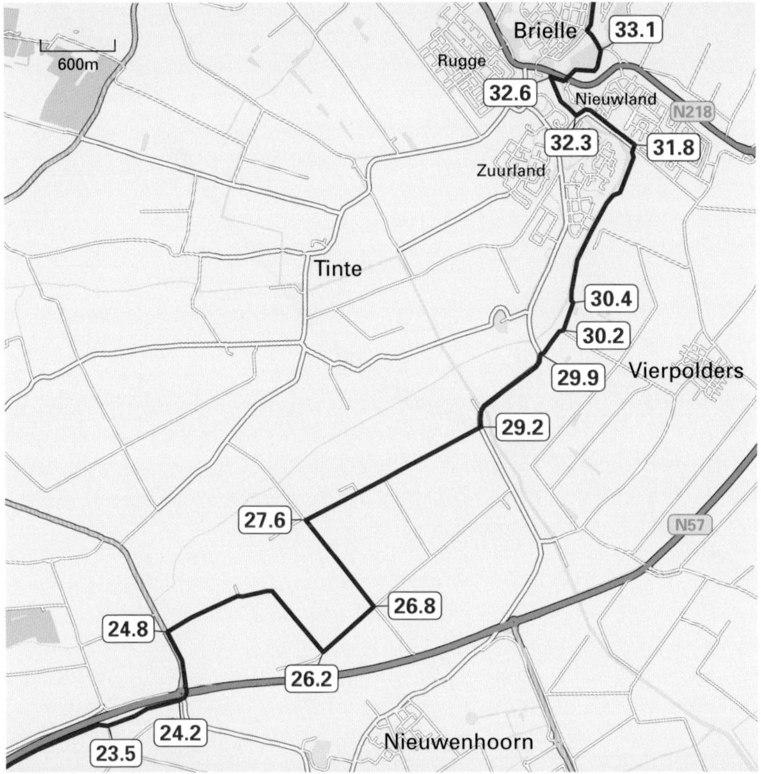

33.3 ⬷ ⌂ 🏨 📷 🍴 ✝ **Brielle**
(town centre ↑)

33.3 Before bridge 1st rd →
(Slagveld) 🚗

33.8 2nd bridge ←, after bridge
→ (to Centrum) 🚗

34.0 1st bridge →, after bridge
→ (Maarland NZ, to
Oostvoorne, later Rochus
Meeuwiszoonweg)

34.4 Join 🚲 on right-hand side
(Brielsemeerroute)

34.7 At KP 26 ← via "fietspad"
(Brielsemeerpad, to
Oostvoorne & KP 53), keep
going ↑

37.8 📷 🍴 **De Kogeloven** (pavilion
in park)

38.6 At jct of KP 53 → (Gorslaan,
to KP 52)

39.4 At jct ⬉ via rd through holiday
park area (to KP 52)

40.7 At T-jct of KP 52 → via 🚲 on
right-hand side (to Europoort
& KP 54)

41.5 1st 🚲 ← (to Europoort)

41.7 At T-jct ← via 🚲 on left-hand
side (to Europoort)

41.8 Jct in front of main rd, end
of route
- For Hook of Holland ↑ via
  🚲 (to Hoek van Holland),
  this is same jct as after
  6.1 km on route towards
  Hook of Holland on
  page 41.
- For Ferry Terminal to Hull
  → via 🚲 (to Europoort),
  this is same jct as after
  13.4 km on route towards
  Ferry Terminal Hull on
  page 41.

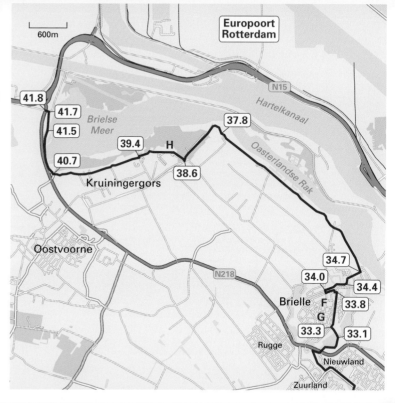

Accommodation Listings

Route section & map ref			Town	Type	Name and address	Phone	Internet
1	Link IJmuiden	A	IJmuiden	▲	De Duindoorn, Badweg 40	+ 31 255 510773	www.duindoorn.nl
1	Link IJmuiden	B	IJmuiden	▲	De Heerenduinen, Heerenduinweg 4	+ 31 255 515933	–
1	Link IJmuiden	C	IJmuiden	⌂	Gastenverblijf IJmuiden, Wijk aan Zeeerweg 76	+ 31 255 510037	–
1	Link IJmuiden	D	IJmuiden	⌂	Janets B&B, Valereniusstraat 3	+ 31 6 54758801	www.janetsbedandbreakfast.nl
1	Link IJmuiden	E	Driehuis	⌂	B&B Noordzee, PC Hooftlaan 11	+ 31 255 540433	www.bbnoordzee.nl
1	Link IJmuiden	F	Santpoort Noord	⌂	De Zanderij, Duin en Kruidbergerweg 24	+ 31 235 373141	–
1	Link IJmuiden	G	Santpoort Noord	⌂	De Jachtkamer, Duin en Kruidbergergweg 76	+ 31 235 371558	www.dejachtkamer.com
3	Main Circular	A	Hoek van Holland	⌂	Pension Seinpad, Seinpad 21	+ 31 174 385652	www.seinpad.nl
3	Main Circular	B	Hoek van Holland	⌂	Langeslag B&B, Prins Hendrikstraat 190a	+ 31 6 42402237	http://home.kpn.nl/langeslagbb
3	Main Circular	C	Hoek van Holland	⌂	't Seepaerd, Harwichweg 210	+ 31 174 383331	www.seepaerd.nl
3	Main Circular	D	Hoek van Holland	⌂	Hotel Noordzee, Dirk van den Burgweg 69	+ 31 174 382273	hotel-noordzee.com
3	Main Circular	E	s' Gravenzande	▲	Jagtveld, Nieuwlandsedijk 41, s' Gravenzande	+ 31 174 413479	www.jagtveld.nl
3	Main Circular	F	s' Gravenzande	⛺	Vlugtenburg Trekvogel basic huts, 't Louwtje 10	+ 31 174 412420	www.vlugtenburg.nl
3	Main Circular	G	Ter Heyde	⌂	B&B Linda, Duinstraat 86	+ 31 174 242069	www.bedandbreakfastlinda.nl
3	Main Circular	H	Ter Heyde	▲	De Molenslag, Molenslag 2	+ 31 174 240449	www.campingdemolenslag.com
4	Main Circular	A	Den Haag	⌂	Sweens B&B, Statenlaan 60	+ 31 70 3545781	http://filasoft.nl/sweens/index.html
4	Main Circular	B	Den Haag	⌂	Polls B&B, Malakkastraat 14	+ 31 70 3503785	http://polls-bedandbreakfast.nl
4	Main Circular	C	Den Haag	⛺	StayOkay Den Haag, Scheepmakersstraat 27	+ 31 70 3157877	www.stayokay.com
4	Main Circular	D	Den Haag	⌂	Four Seasons, Leuvensestraat 56	+ 31 70 3552118	www.hotel4seasons.com
5	Main Circular	A	Katwijk	⌂	Hotel van Beelen, Wilhelminstraat 10-12	+ 31 71 4073333	www.hotelvanbeelen.nl
5	Main Circular	B	Katwijk	⌂	Bed and Breakfast aan Zee, Emmastraat 11	+ 31 6 636026993	www.bbaanzee.nl
5	Main Circular	C	Katwijk	⌂	Hotel Savoy, Boulevard 1	+ 31 71 4015645	www.hotelsavoy.nl
5	Main Circular	D	Noordwijk	⌂	Pension Maaike, Quarles van Uffordstraat 96	+ 31 6 25255907	www.pensionmaaike.nl
5	Main Circular	E	Noordwijk	⌂	De Driesprong, Quarles van Uffordstraat 4	+ 31 71 3613487	www.pensiondedriesprong.nl
5	Main Circular	F	Noordwijk	⌂	De Zonnester, Prins Bernhardstraat 23	+ 31 71 3615958	www.pensiondezonnester.nl
5	Main Circular-link	G	Noordwijkerhout	⛺	StayOkay Noordwijk, Langevelderlaan 45	+ 31 252 372920	www.stayokay.com
5	Main Circular-link	H	Noordwijkerhout	▲	Noordwijkse Duinen, Kappeleboslaan 41	+ 31 252 372485	www.noordwijkseduinen.nl
5	Main Circular-link	I	Noordwijkerhout	▲	Sollasi, Duinschooten 14	+ 31 252 376437	www.sollasi.nl
5	Main Circular	J	Zandvoort	⌂	Pension Corper, Koninginneweg 21	+ 31 23 5713449	www.corper.eu
5	Main Circular	K	Zandvoort	⌂	Pension Schier, Hogeweg 45	+ 31 23 5719541	www.pensionschier.eu
5	Main Circular	L	Zandvoort	⌂	Pension De Meeuw, Hogeweg 50	+ 31 23 5320393	www.pensiondemeeuw.nl

Route section & map ref			Town	Type	Name and address	Phone	Internet
5	Main Circular	M	Bloemendaal	▲	De Lakens, Zeeweg 60	+ 31 23 5411570	www.kennemerduincampings.nl
6	Main Circular	A	Haarlem	⌂	Malts Hotel, Zijlstraat 56-58	+ 31 23 5512385	www.maltshotel.nl
6	Main Circular	B	Haarlem	⌂	Carillon Hotel, Grote Markt 27	+ 31 23 5310591	www.hotelcarillon.nl
6	Main Circular	C	Haarlem	⌂	Die Raeckse, Raaks 1-3	+ 31 23 5326629	www.die-raeckse.nl
6	Main Circular	D	Haarlem	⌂	Bot B&B, Raamsingel 40	+ 31 23 5423160	www.botbedbreakfast.com
6	Main Circular	E	Haarlem	⌂	Hotel Amadeus, Grote Markt 10	+ 31 23 5324530	www.amadeus-hotel.com
7	Tulips Route	A	Voorhout	⌂	Boerhaave, Herenstraat 57	+ 31 252 211483	www.hotelboerhaave.nl
7	Tulips Route	B	Lisse	⌂	De Nachtegaal, Heereweg 10	+ 31 252 433030	www.nachtegaal.nl
8	Main Circular	A	Haarlem	⌂⌂	StayOkay Haarlem, Jan Gijzenpad 3	+ 31 23 5373793	www.stayokay.com
8	Main Circular	B	Koog a/d Zaan	⌂	Zaanse Koopmanshuis, Lagedijk 52-54	+ 31 75 6310239	www.zaansekoopmanshuis.nl
9	Main Circular	A	Amsterdam	⌂	Amstel Botel, NSDM-Pier 3	+ 31 20 6264247	www.amstelbotel.nl
9	Main Circular	B	Amsterdam	⌂⌂	StayOkay Stadsdoelen, Kloveniersburgwal 97	+ 31 20 6246832	www.stayokay.com
9	Main Circular	C	Amsterdam	⌂⌂	StayOkay Vondelpark, Zandpad 5	+ 31 20 5898996	www.stayokay.com
10	Main Circular	A	Amsterdam	⌂⌂	StayOkay Zeeburg, Timorplein 21	+ 31 20 5513190	www.stayokay.com
10	Main Circular	B	Weesp	⌂	Hart van Weesp, Herengracht 35	+ 31 294 419353	www.hartvanweesp.nl
10	Main Circular	C	Vreeland	⌂	De Willigen, Nigtevechtseweg 186-188	+ 31 6 51798045	www.dewilligenlogies.nl
10	Main Circular	D	Loenen	▲⌂⌂	Fort Spion (also basic huts), Bloklaan 9 (N403)	+ 31 294 234932	www.fortspion.nl
10	Main Circular	E	Breukelen	⌂	B&B Breukelen, Zandpad 83	+ 31 346 261201	www.bnb-breukelen.eu
11	Main Circular	A	Oud Zuilen	⌂	Klein Zuylenburg, Dorpsstraat 1	+ 31 6 20738375	www.kleinzuylenburg.nl
11	Main Circular	B	Utrecht	⌂	Hotel Oorspongpark, F.C. Dondersstraat 12	+ 31 30 2716303	www.oorsprongpark.nl
11	Main Circular	C	Utrecht	⌂	Den Ulch, Westerkade 8a	+ 31 30 2400696	www.martschellekensdesign.nl/denulch
11	Main Circular	D	Utrecht	⌂	Kilim Centre Inn, Herenweg 28 bis	+ 31 30 2334975	www.kilim-centre-inn.nl
11	Main Circular	E	Utrecht	⌂	B&B Herenweg, Herenweg 32	+ 31 6 22692124	www.bedandbreakfasthello.nl
11	Main Circular	F	Utrecht	⌂	Kanne, Looierstraat 23	+ 31 6 28766744	www.appartement-kanne.nl
12	Main Circular	A	De Haar	⌂▲	Boerderij Hazenveld, Laag-Nieuwkoop 36	+ 31 30 6663372	www.boerderijhazenveld.nl
12	Main Circular	B	Woerden	⌂	Bed & Brood Groenendaal, Groenendaal 7	+ 31 348 402825	www.bedenbroodgroenendaal.nl
12	Main Circular	C	Snelrewaard	▲	Oude Boomgaard, Zuid-Linschoterzandweg 31	+ 31 348 560071	www.oude-boomgaard.nl
12	Main Circular	D	Snelrewaard	⌂	De Boerderij, Zuid-Linschoterzandweg 15	+ 31 348 421199	www.bedandbreakfastthefarm.com
12	Main Circular	E	Oudewater	⌂	Abrona, Broeckerstraat 20	+ 31 348 567466	www.hotelabrona.nl
12	Main Circular	F	Haastrecht	⌂	B&B Providentia, Steinsedijk 55	+ 31 182 501829	www.bbprovidentia.nl
12	Main Circular	G	Gouda	⌂	B&B De Bovenetage, Vijverstraat 7	+ 31 182 512794	www.bovenetage.nl
12	Main Circular	H	Gouda	⌂	De Utrechtse Dom, Geuzenstraat 6	+ 31 182 528833	www.hotelgouda.nl
12	Main Circular	I	Gouda	⌂	Hotel Keizerskroon, Keizerstraat 11-13	+ 31 182 528096	www.hotelkeizerskroon.nl

Route section & map ref			Town	Type	Name and address	Phone	Internet
13	Main Circular	A	Zevenhuizen	▲	De Koornmolen, Tweemanspolder 6a	+ 31 180 631654	www.koornmolen.nl
13	Main Circular	B	Delft	▲	De Grutto, Abtswoude 27a	+ 31 6 510 10162	www.degrutto.eu
13	Main Circular	C	Delft	⌂	De Vlaming, Vlamingstraat 52	+ 31 15 2132127	www.hoteldevlaming.nl
13	Main Circular	D	Delft	⌂	De Emauspoort, Vrouwenregt 9-11	+ 31 15 2190219	www.emauspoort.nl
13	Main Circular	E	Delft	⌂	De Koophandel, Beestenmarkt 30	+ 31 15 2142302	www.hoteldekoophandel.nl
13	Main Circular	F	Delft	⌂	De Ark, Koornmarkt 65	+ 31 15 2157999	www.deark.nl
15	Northern Route	A	Amsterdam	▲	Vliegenbos, Meeuwenlaan 138	+ 31 20 636 8855	www.vliegenbos.com
15	Northern Route	B	Uitdam	▲	Uitdam, Zeedijk 2	+ 31 20 4031433	www.campinguitdam.nl
15	Northern Route	C	Marken	⌂	Hof van Marken, Buurt 2, Nr 15	+ 31 299 601300	www.hofvanmarken.nl
15	Northern Route	D	Monnickendam	▲	Hemmeland, Hemmeland 1	+ 31 299 655555	www.hemmeland.nl
16	Northern Route	A	Volendam	⌂	Old Dutch, Haven 142	+ 31 299 399888	www.olddutch.nl
16	Northern Route	B	Volendam	⌂	Naomi's Pension House, Ventersgracht 11	+ 31 299 367100	–
16	Northern Route	C	Volendam	⌂	B&B Doortje, Hofstede 1	+ 31 299 364539	–
16	Northern Route	D	Edam	⌂	De Fortuna, Spuistraat 3	+ 31 299 371671	www.fortuna-edam.nl
16	Northern Route	E	Edam	⌂	De Harmonie, Voorhaven 92-94	+ 31 299 371664	www.harmonie-edam.nl
16	Northern Route	F	Edam	⌂	B&B Edam, Tonissenstraat 14	+ 31 6 14433959	www.benb-edam.nl
16	Northern Route	G	Middelie	⌂	Wapen van Middelie, Brink 1	+ 31 299 621376	www.hetwapenvanmiddelie.nl
16	Northern Route	H	Oosthuizen	⌂	Zonneweelde, Oosteinde 87a	+ 31 299 401317	www.zonneweelde.nl
16	Northern Route	I	Schardam	▲	De Eenhoorn, Burgerwoudweg 1	+ 31 6 53798020	www.campingdeeenhoorn.nl
17	Northern Route	A	Hoorn	⌂	Petit Nord, Kleine Noord 53-55	+ 31 229 212750	www.hotelpetitnord.nl
17	Northern Route	B	Hoorn	⌂	Keizerskroon, Breed 33	+ 31 229 212717	www.keizerskroonhoorn.nl
17	Northern Route	C	Hoorn	⌂	De Magneet, Kleine Oost 5	+ 31 229 215021	www.hoteldemagneet.nl
17	Northern Route	D	Hoorn	⌂	De Posthoorn, Breed 25/27	+ 31 229 214057	www.herbergdeposthoorn.nl
17	Northern Route	E	Schellinkhout	⌂	De Munnickay, Zuiderdijk 60a	+ 31 229 210390	www.zuidwest7.nl
17	Northern Route	F	Schellinkhout	▲	De Appelhoek, Zuiderdijk 46 (Wijdenes)	+ 31 229 501150	www.appelhoek.nl
17	Northern Route	G	Enkhuizen	▲	De Vest, Noorderweg 31	+ 31 228 321221	www.campingdevest.nl
17	Northern Route	H	Enkhuizen	⌂	De Koepoort, Westerstraat 294	+ 31 228 314966	www.dekoepoort.nl
17	Northern Route	I	Enkhuizen	⌂	Wapen van Enkhuizen, Breedstraat 59	+ 31 228 313434	www.wapenvanenkhuizen.nl
17	Northern Route	J	Enkhuizen	⌂	Bij de buren, Bagijnestraat 6	+ 31 228 315136	www.overnachtenbijdeburen.nl
17	Northern Route	K	Enkhuizen	⌂	B&B Enkhuizen, Van Loosenpark 1	+ 31 228 315469	www.bedandbreakfastenkhuizen.nl
17	Northern Route	L	Lelystad	⌂	Het Boshuys, Uilenweg 3	+ 31 320 218581	–
17	Northern Route	M	Almere	▲	De Kemphaan, Kemphaanpad 10	+ 31 36 5384417	–
17	Northern Route	N	Almere	⌂	Pension Almere, Lindengouw 70	+ 31 6 46446409	www.pensionalmere.nl

Route section & map ref			Town	Type	Name and address	Phone	Internet
18	Eastern Route	A	Soest	⌂	Paleis om de hoek, Dorresteinweg 74	+ 31 6 53963016	www.paleisomdehoek.nl
18	Eastern Route	B	Soest	⌂	Buitengewoon Soest, Veenzoom 6	+ 31 35 6011555	www.bbsoest.nl
18	Eastern Route	C	Soest	🏠	StayOkay Soest, Bosstraat 16	+ 31 35 6012296	www.stayokay.com
18	Eastern Route	D	Soest	▲	De Eerste Aanleg, De Zoom 7	+ 31 35 6011327	http://eerste.aanleg.vakantieland.nl
19	Eastern Route	A	Maarn	⌂	Stameren, Amersfoortseweg 1a	+ 31 343 443122	www.bedandbreakfast-stameren.nl
19	Eastern Route	B	Doorn	⌂	Boschzicht, Mesdaglaan 11	+ 31 6 81152315	www.bbdoorn.nl
19	Eastern Route	C	Doorn	⌂	B&B Doorn, Acacialaan 10	+ 31 343 413191	www.bedandbreakfastdoorn.nl
19	Eastern Route	D	Leersum	⌂	De Darthuizer Molen, Molenweg 1	+ 31 6 24176637	www.darthuizermolen.nl
19	Eastern Route	E	Leersum	⌂	Het hofje van Lies, Traaiweg 12	+ 31 343 452915	www.hethofjevanlies.nl
19	Eastern Route	F	Amerongen	⌂	De Utrechtse Heuvelrug, Wilhelminaweg 52a	+ 31 343 461051	http://amerongen.greup.com
19	Eastern Route	G	Amerongen	⌂	Buitenlust, H. v.d. Boschstraat	+ 31 343 451692	www.buitenlust-amerongen.nl
19	Eastern Route	H	Elst	🏠	StayOkay Elst, Veenendaalsestraatweg 65	+ 31 318 472460	www.stayokay.com
20	Eastern Route	A	Kesteren	▲ ⌂	Den Ouden Dam, Hoge Dijkseweg 19	+ 31 6 26963380	www.denoudendam.nl
20	Eastern Route	B	Rhenen	⌂	Wapen van Rhenen, Herenstraat 75	+ 31 317 311112	www.hotelrhenen.nl
20	Eastern Route	C	Rhenen	⌂	't Paviljoen, Grebbeweg 103	+ 31 317 619003	www.paviljoen.nl
20	Eastern Route	D	Opheusden	⌂	't Veerhuis, Veerweg 1	+ 31 488 441207	www.veerhuis-opheusden.nl
20	Eastern Route	E	Slijk-Ewijk	⌂	De Remketting, Clara Fabriciuspark 15	+ 31 481 481737	www.deremketting.nl
20	Eastern Route	F	Oosterhout	▲	De Grote Altena, Waaldijk 39	+ 31 481 481200	www.campingdegrotealtena.nl
20	Eastern Route	G	Oosterhout	⌂	Buitenwaard, Dijkstraat 10	+ 31 481 481832	www.buitenwaard.nl
21	Eastern Route	A	Nijmegen	⌂	B&B Wilhelmina, Wilhelminasingel 36	+ 31 24 3233687	www.bedandbreakfastnijmegen.com
21	Eastern Route	B	Nijmegen	⌂	De Kleine Prins, Bijleveldsingel 9	+ 31 6 55773080	–
21	Eastern Route	C	Nijmegen	⌂	De Amuse, Lange Hazelstraat 64	+ 31 24 3245570	www.deamuse.nl
21	Eastern Route	D	Nijmegen	⌂	Pollux, Biezenstraat 7	+ 31 24 3787426	www.bedandbreakfast-nijmegen.nl
21	Eastern Route	E	Nijmegen	⌂	City Park Hotel, Hertogstraat 1	+ 31 24 3220498	www.cityparkhotel.nl
21	Eastern Route	F	Nijmegen	⌂	Atlanta Hotel, Grote Markt 38-40	+ 31 24 3603000	www.atlanta-hotel.nl
21	Eastern Route	G	Beek	⌂	't Spijker, Rijksstraatweg 191	+ 31 24 6841295	www.hotelspijker.nl
21	Eastern Route	H	Berg en Dal	▲	De Groote Vlierenberg, Zevenheuvelenweg 57	+ 31 24 6841481	www.campingdegrootevlierenberg.nl
21	Eastern Route	I	Berg en Dal	▲	Nederrijkswald, Zevenheuvelenweg 47	+ 31 24 6841782	www.nederrijkswald.nl
21	Eastern Route	J	Groesbeek	▲	De Oude Molen, Wylerbaan 2a	+ 31 24 3971715	www.oudemolen.nl
22	Southern Route	A	Vlissingen	⌂	Pension Marijke, Coosje Buskenstraat 88	+ 31 118 415062	www.pensionmarijke.nl
22	Southern Route	B	Vlissingen	⌂	Pension Louisiana, Nieuwendijk 25	+ 31 118 413554	–
22	Southern Route	C	Vlissingen	⌂	Pension Wolf, Aagje Dekenstraat 95	+ 31 118 414797	www.hotelpensionwolff.nl
22	Southern Route	D	Vlissingen	⌂	De Rode Boei, Singel 104	+ 31 118 411577	www.derodeboei.nl

Route section & map ref			Town	Type	Name and address	Phone	Internet
22	Southern Route	E	Vlissingen	⌂	B&B Vlissingen, Nieuwstraat 25	+ 31 118 414797	www.bedandbreakfast-vlissingen.nl
22	Southern Route	F	Dishoek	⌂	Pension Duinlust, Dishoek 18	+ 31 118 551534	www.duinlust.info
22	Southern Route	G	Zoutelande	▲	De Meerpaal, Werendijkseweg 14	+ 31 118 561300	www.ardoer.com
22	Southern Route	H	Zoutelande	⌂	Klein Zomerlust, Pauwtje 4	+ 31 6 51154200	www.everyoneweb.com/kleinzomerlust.nl •
22	Southern Route	I	Zoutelande	⌂	Dune Hotel Valkenhof, Zuidstraat 9-11	+ 31 118 561252	www.hotelvalkenhof.nl
22	Southern Route	J	Zoutelande	⌂	Duinhotel Haga, Westkapelseweg 17	+ 31 118 561823	www.duinhotelhaga.nl
22	Southern Route	K	Westkapelle	⌂	Pieter de Coninck, Noordkerkepad 10a-12	+ 31 118 571393	www.hotelwestkapelle.nl
22	Southern Route	L	Westkapelle	⌂	De Valk, Zuidstraat 97	+ 31 118 571294	www.hrdevalk.nl
22	Southern Route	M	Westkapelle	⌂	Zuidoost Zakelijk, Noordstraat 57a	+ 31 118 571012	www.vakantiebijzuidoost.nl
22	Southern Route	N	Domburg	▲	Noordduin, Schelpweg 17a	+ 31 118 582666	www.campingnoordduin.nl
22	Southern Route	O	Domburg	▲	't Veldhof, Trommelweg 4	+ 31 118 582557	www.veldehof.nl
22	Southern Route	P	Domburg	⌂	De Lijsterhof, Weststraat 11a+ 11b	+ 31 118 750223	www.delijsterhof.nl
22	Southern Route	Q	Domburg	⌂	Bos en Zee, Nehalleniaweg 8	+ 31 118 581452	www.hotelboschenzee.nl
22	Southern Route	R	Domburg	⌂	Vierwegen, 't Groentje 10	+ 31 118 583393	www.vierwegen.nl
22	Southern Route	S	Domburg	🏠	StayOkay Domburg, Duinvlietweg 8	+ 31 118 581254	www.stayokay.com
22	Southern Route	T	Breezand	▲	Oranjezon, Koningin Emmaweg 16a	+ 31 118 591549	www.oranjezon.nl
23	Southern Route	A	Breezand	▲	Schorre, Vroondijk 2	+ 31 118 594473	www.schorre.nl
23	Southern Route	B	Breezand	⌂	Duinoord, Breezand 65	+ 31 118 591346	www.hotel-duinoord.nl
23	Southern Route	C	Burgh-Haamstede	▲	Veldvreugd, Brabersweg 5	+ 31 111 651225	–
23	Southern Route	D	Burgh-Haamstede	⌂	De Lindehof, Julianastraat 21	+ 31 111 651834	www.pensiondelindehof.nl
23	Southern Route	E	Burgh-Haamstede	⌂	Hotel Bom, Noordstraat 2	+ 31 111 652229	www.hotel-bom.nl
23	Southern Route	F	Burgh-Haamstede	▲	Groenoord-Boomgaard, Vertonsweg 2	+ 31 111 653672	–
23	Southern Route	G	Burgh-Haamstede	▲	De Duinhoeve, Maireweg 7	+ 31 111 651562	www.deduinhoeve.nl
23	Southern Route	H	Renesse	⌂	De Zeeuwse Stromen, Duinwekken 5	+ 31 111 462040	www.zeeuwsestromen.nl
23	Southern Route	I	Renesse	⌂	Zeerust, Rampweg 1	+ 31 111 461390	www.pcrzeerust.nl
24	Southern Route	A	Ouddorp	⌂	Pension Ouddorp, Dorpsweg 26	+ 31 187 681724	www.pensionouddorp.nl
24	Southern Route	B	Ouddorp	⌂	Akershoek, Boompjes 1	+ 31 187 681437	www.hotelakershoek.nl
24	Southern Route	C	Ouddorp	⌂	De Smousenhoek, Hazersweg 23	+ 31 6 21221410	www.desmousenhoek.nl
24	Southern Route	D	Goedereede	⌂	De Gouden Leeuw, Markt 11	+ 31 187 491371	www.pensionouddorp.nl
24	Southern Route	E	Havenhoofd	⌂	Haveneind, Haveneind 1	+ 31 187 750772	www.haveneind.nl
24	Southern Route	F	Brielle	⌂	De Nymph, Voorstraat 45	+ 31 181 415230	www.hotelbrielle.nl
24	Southern Route	G	Brielle	⌂	De Zalm, Voorstraat 6-8	+ 31 347 750436	www.hoteldezalm.nl
24	Southern Route	H	Kruiningergors	▲	Kruiningergors, Gorsplein 2	+ 31 181 482711	www.molecaten.nl